Adoption

and

Ethics

A SERIES BY MADELYN FREUNDLICH

THE ROLE OF RACE, CULTURE, AND NATIONAL ORIGIN IN ADOPTION

CHILD WELFARE LEAGUE OF AMERICA

THE EVAN B. DONALDSON ADOPTION INSTITUTE

The Child Welfare League of America (CWLA), the nation's oldest and largest membership-based child welfare organization, is committed to engaging all Americans in promoting the well-being of children and protecting every child from harm.

CHILD WELFARE LEAGUE OF AMERICA, INC.
440 First Street, NW, Third Floor, Washington, DC 20001-2085
E-mail: books@cwla.org

CURRENT PRINTING (last digit)
10 9 8 7 6 5 4 3 2 1

Cover design by James Melvin
Text design by Peggy Porter Tierney

Printed in the United States of America

ISBN # 0–87868–797–1

Library of Congress Cataloging-in-Publication Data
Freundlich, Madelyn.
  The role of race, culture, and national origin in adoption/Madelyn Freundlich.
    p. cm.
  Includes bibliographical references.
  ISBN 0-87868-797-1 (alk. paper)
  1. Interracial adoptioni--United States. 2. Intercountry adoption--United States. I. Title.
HV875.64 .F74 2000
362.73'4'0973--dc21

                                                                                    00-033689

Contents

Preface

This title is the first in a series of publications developed by the Evan B. Donaldson Adoption Institute and published by CWLA Press. The series is part of the Adoption Institute's multiyear initiative focused on ethical issues in adoption. It is designed to provide the field with a synthesis of the current knowledge base on key adoption policy and practice issues—issues that currently pose challenges to adoption professionals and are likely to confront the field in the future. This examination of the role of race, culture, and national origin in adoption introduces the series of four such publications, with books on the following topics forthcoming: the impact of adoption on members of the adoption triad; market forces in adoption; and adoption and the reproductive technologies.

Why a Focus on Ethics in Adoption

Adoption is a complex subject, with social, psychological, legal, and cultural dimensions. It is shaped by policy—at the international, national, state, county, and agency levels—and by practice—on the part of social workers, attorneys, judges, mental health professionals, and others. It involves the needs, interests, and rights of children, birth parents, relatives, foster parents, adoptive parents, and adult adoptees. Adoption includes domestic adoptions of healthy newborns, international adoptions of children from dozens of countries with widely varying policies, and adoptions of children in foster care in this country. Because of this complexity, adoption has been and continues to be the subject of much debate. The controversies in adoption have extended across a spectrum of policy and practice issues, and although the contentious issues have become clear, resolution has not been achieved nor has consensus developed regarding a framework on which to further quality adoption policy and practice.

Productive outcomes have been hindered by the constituency-based considerations that have shaped, to a great extent, the tenor of the debate. Emotion and rhetoric have come to characterize much of the discussion and, as a result, it has been difficult to focus on substantive issues in a reasoned and informed manner or clarify the goals and principles that can assist in resolving the many points of disagreement. From the divisive debates on access to identifying information, to the emotionally-laden controversies on transracial adoption, to the increasingly intense disputes over the competing "rights" of members of the adoption triad—the environment surrounding adoption has become highly charged, and focused efforts to craft quality policy and practice more difficult to achieve.

The Adoption Institute, in collaboration with leading thinkers in the field of adoption from across the country, approached this environment by proposing an ethics-based framework for analyzing and resolving the complex challenges in adoption. The decision to utilize an ethics-based approach was based, first, on a belief that ethics could provide a method for reframing the critical issues in adoption and avoiding the divisiveness that has impeded the resolution of the key challenges. Second, the choice of an ethics-based approach was based on an assessment that such a framework would support the identification of the range of issues that impact contemporary adoption, the analysis of relevant considerations from multiple perspectives, and the development of a course of action for improving future policy and practice. The Adoption Institute's ethics initiative has three major components:

- an identification and examination of the core values and principles that underlie quality adoption policy and practice;

- thorough analyses of the critical policy and practice issues that demand attention; and

- the development of a strategy that draws on a sound knowledge base to advance quality adoption policy and practice in the future.

The Critical Issues in Adoption

Because adoption is complex, bringing to the fore many competing interests, values, perspectives, and constituencies, it is not an easy task to reach consensus on which issues represent the most critical questions. The Adoption Institute approached this challenging process by first bringing together a multidisciplinary Ethics Advisory Committee. The members of this group represent a rich diversity of professional backgrounds and expertise, including adoption practice and policy, clinical psychology, sociology, political science, the law, the judiciary, bioethics, medicine, medical anthropology, religion, and social science research. With the guidance of this Committee, the Adoption Institute identified key ethical issues that affect adoption policy and practice and prioritized the most critical issues for in-depth analysis and action. The following topics were selected as critical areas for ongoing attention and work.

The Role of Race, Culture, and National Origin in Adoption

This topic considers critical questions regarding the role of race, culture, and national origin in adoption from the perspective of individuals served by adoption and from a broad policy perspective. In this complex area of adoption policy and practice, there are many unresolved questions related to the role of race, culture, and national origin in an adoptee's personal identity and the extent to which racial and cultural similarities and differences between adoptive parents and children should be taken into account. These questions have been placed at the forefront of the policy debate as a result of recent changes in federal law—which now prohibits consideration of race and culture in the adoptive placement of children in foster care; debates related to the Indian Child Welfare Act; and the mandates of the Hague Convention on Intercountry Adoption.

The Impact of Adoption on Adopted Persons, Birth Parents, Adoptive Parents, and Adoptive Families

This topic focuses on the many ways that adoption may impact each member of the adoption triad. For the adopted person, adoption may affect the individual's overall adjustment and well-being, as well as the ability to develop a personal identity. What are the outcomes for adopted persons and to what extent do past and current adoption practices affect those outcomes? For the birth parent, adoption practice and law may impact, both in the short and long term, an individual's sense of personal integrity. To what extent are birth parents well served by adoption and how do societal perceptions of birth parents affect their sense of well-being? For adoptive parents, adoption involves achieving parenthood in a nontraditional way. To what extent does being "approved" to parent impact adoptive parents? Do adoptive families face special challenges in a society that accords primacy to biological bonds?

The Market Forces in Adoption

This topic considers various aspects of the "business" of adoption in terms of market factors. With the shifting demographics of infant adoption, international adoption, and special needs adoption, issues are raised about the role of money in adoption, who holds the "power" in adoption, and to whom adoption professionals are accountable. Increasingly, the field of adoption struggles with such questions as: To what extent has there been a commodification of children who are placed with adoptive families? How is the adoption process regulated and by whom? How are the roles of birth and adoptive parents affected by differences in resources? Is the concept of accountability relevant to adoption, and if so, how? Do market forces undermine ethical adoption practice?

Adoption and Reproductive Technology

This fourth topic raises the question of whether reproductive technologies (including sperm donation, egg donation, and embryo implantation), which may or may not provide a child genetically connected to one or both parents, create a situation that is analogous to adoption. Should the knowledge that has been acquired in the field of adoption be applied in the area of reproductive technologies? Are issues in adoption—such as identity, access to background information, and search—equally applicable in the context of reproductive technology? Should any or all adoption practice standards apply in reproductive technologies?

The Series

Essential to knowledgeable discussion and issue resolution in each of these four areas is a sound understanding of the current knowledge base—the research, the practice-based knowledge, and the policy analyses advanced by leading thinkers in the many fields bearing on adoption: social work, law, psychology, child and adolescent development, medicine, and education. The books in this series are designed to provide a synthesis of the existing knowledge base that can inform and challenge thinking and analysis in each of the critical topic areas. They outline the key issues; review the current data, including statistical information to the extent it exists; identify the research that addresses the key issues; describe the current practice-based knowledge; and synthesize the policy arguments that have been advanced and debated. Whenever possible, the strengths and weaknesses of various perspectives are assessed.

The books in this series, including this title on the role of race, culture, and national origin in adoption, are not designed to take a position on the issues or advance a specific viewpoint as to what is "ethical" or "unethical." It is only through ongoing discussion that consensus can be reached as to what represents the most ethical course of action in adoption—for those directly touched by adoption and for those who provide professional adoption services. It is hoped that the series will provide a tool for furthering this discussion—a springboard for advancing adoption policy and practice currently and into the future.

Acknowledgments

The Adoption Institute wishes to thank The Hite Foundation for its generous support of the Institute's work on the role of race, culture, and national origin in adoption and, specifically, the development of this publication. The commitment of The Hite Foundation to child welfare issues made the Institute's work on this critical issue possible.

The Adoption Institute also acknowledges a number of individuals who provided assistance in the development of this publication on the role of race, culture, and national origin in adoption. The following individuals generously gave of their time and expertise in reviewing drafts and offered critical guidance and suggestions: Susan Soon-Keum Cox, Vice President of Public Policy & External Affairs, Holt International Children's Services, Eugene, OR; Dr. Diana Edwards, Professor of Anthropology, Silver City, NM: Susan Freivalds, Coordinator of Hague Convention Policy, Joint Council on International Children's Services, Washington, DC; Maureen Heffernan, Adoption Consultant, Kent, Ohio; Michelle Hester, Director, International Adoption Program, The Barker Foundation, Cabin John, MD; Professor Ruth-Arlene W. Howe, Boston College Law School, Newton Centre, MA; Dr. Ruth McRoy, School of Social Work, University of Texas at Austin, Austin, TX; Dr. Robert Ortega, School of Social Work, University of Michigan, Ann Arbor, MI; Marilyn St. Germaine, Indigenous Nations Child and Family Services, Oakland, CA; Ann Sullivan, Director of Adoption Services, Child Welfare League of America, Washington, DC; and Judge William Thorne, Salt Lake City, UT.

The editorial assistance of Leigh Nowicki, Program Assistant at The Evan B. Donaldson Adoption Institute, is also gratefully acknowledged. Ms. Nowicki's ongoing support and expertise were essential to the completion of this work. Appreciation is also expressed for the research assistance of Aline Kahn, Jackie Cunningham, and Kaerensa Kraft.

Madelyn Freundlich, Executive Director
The Evan B. Donaldson Adoption Institute

Introduction

Among the most pressing issues confronting adoption, both domestically and internationally, are considerations related to race, culture, and national origin. What role do race and culture currently play in adoption? To what extent has adoption, as a service for children and families, been shaped by racial and cultural considerations in the past, and to what extent should considerations related to race and culture shape adoption practice and policy in the future? On the international front, how should considerations related to national origin, in addition to race and culture, be addressed?

These complex issues are examined here from several perspectives. First, the difficulties presented by efforts to define the concepts of "race," "culture," and "ethnicity" and the relationship of these concepts to "national origin" are explored. The historical context for a consideration of the role of race, culture, and national origin in adoption is briefly described. The complex issues bearing on the role of race and culture in the adoption of children are addressed in three parts: first, considerations related to race and culture in the adoption of children in foster care in the U.S.; second, the issue of culture as it relates to the adoption of American Indian children in this country; and third, the role of race, culture, and national origin in international adoption.

The Concepts of Race, Culture, Ethnicity, and National Origin

Any effort to explore the role of race, culture, and national origin in adoption necessitates some understanding of the meaning of these concepts. That understanding, however, is complicated by the reality that consensus is lacking as to what these terms mean. Are "race" and "culture" the same or different concepts? Are these

1

terms synonymous with "ethnicity"? And how does "national origin" relate to "race" and "culture"? The literature reflects wide-ranging use of these terms, and there is ongoing debate regarding appropriate terminology. "Race" and "culture" are treated at times as distinct concepts; in other instances, "culture" and "national origin" are subsumed under the term "ethnicity"; and in yet other circumstances, the terms "race" and "ethnicity" are used inter-changeably [Bernal et al. 1990]. The greater weight of authority appears to favor a view of "race" and "ethnicity"—however "ethnicity" may be defined—as conceptually and experientially distinct concepts [Almaguer 1994; Blauner 1972; Espiritu 1992; Nishi 1989; Omi & Winant 1994; Takaki 1987, 1989; Warner & Srole 1945; Waters 1990, 1992]. Mittelberg and Waters [1992, p. 425], for example, write:

> Race has been used by theorists to refer to distinctions drawn from physical appearance. Ethnicity has been used to refer to distinctions based on national origin, language, religion, food and other cultural markers.

This view, however, is not uniform as one writer has de-scribed "ethnicity" as "cover[ing] groups and organizations based on racial characteristics, tribal bonds, religious affiliation, na-tional origins, as well as cultural distinctiveness" [Khinduka 1995, p.3], a view that merges race, culture and national origin within the single concept of "ethnicity."

Even where there is agreement that "race" refers to physical characteristics and that "ethnicity" refers to attributes other than individuals' outward appearance or phenotype, there is wide divergence on the nature and scope of "ethnicity." Phinney found in a 1990 review of articles addressing "ethnic identity" that the term was variously defined as "self-identification," " feelings of belonging and commitment," a "sense of shared values or atti-tudes," "attitudes toward one's group," and similarities in "lan-guage, behavior, values, and knowledge of ethnic group history" [1990, p.500]—definitions reflecting differing notions of personal identity that in some cases were and in other cases were not group- or culture-based. It may be, however, that "ethnicity" is more commonly associated with culture and national identity, incorporating "language, food, dress, art, music, values, and ways of interacting ... through the roles individuals play ... [and] the ways in which they are expected to express emotions and sentiments" [Cox & Ephross 1998, p.8].

Recognizing that there is a lack of consensus on the use and meanings of these concepts, the terms "race," "culture" and "national origin" are utilized here. Although "race"—referring to physical distinctions among major groups—and "culture"—referring to characteristic patterns of behavior and traditions of groups—may be imprecise terms, "ethnicity" may be even more unclear outside scholarly circles, if indeed "ethnicity" is uniformly defined in the current body of academic writing. Additionally, most child welfare professionals are familiar with the terms "race" and "culture" in relation to policy and practice issues involving adoption and foster care, and the research and practice literature on which this book draws utilize these terms more extensively than the term "ethnicity." "National origin"—referring to the country of one's birth—will be used as an independent concept, distinct from race and culture. It is used, in contrast to "nationality," to avoid confusion between an individual's nationality by birth and his or her nationality as legally and socially established through adoption. "National origin" is of significance in international adoption and may, in some cases, present issues that are distinct from cultural identity.

Even though the terms "race," "culture," and "national origin" may enjoy a greater level of common usage, it is important to note that there remain differences in the application of these terms. The connotations of "race" and "culture" may differ, depending on the reference group. There may be, for example, an underlying assumption that "white" persons—or European Americans—have no meaningful racial identity, nor do they—as opposed to people of color—have a "culture." Some writers have noted that "whites" may, in fact, view themselves as racially neutral or colorless [Tuan, in press; Alba 1990; Frankenberg 1993; Lorde 1984; Waters 1990]. Others, such as McIntosh [1997], suggest that Caucasians may see themselves as the racial norm against which other groups are judged and, therefore, they may avoid the issue of racial identity altogether. "Culture" may likewise have different meanings as applied to "whites" and people of color. Waters [1986, 1990, 1992], for example, observes that Caucasians have the freedom to choose whether they will claim a distinct group identity for themselves and the extent to which they will incorporate the cultural values of that identity into their lives.

By contrast, individuals of color are more likely to define and/ or have their identities defined by race [Omi & Winant 1994]. For racial minority groups, race plays a significant role in shaping perspectives and informing experiences with others [Tuan, in press]. For some communities of color, culture and/or national origin is added to race as a salient aspect of identity [Tuan, in press; Mittelberg & Waters 1992]. For others, culture and/or national origin may be more powerful than race, though some have argued that when individuals are confronted with both a racial identity and a cultural identity, their racial identities almost always prevail [Mittelberg & Waters 1992].

These issues, which raise a host of considerations that are beyond the scope of this book, nevertheless provide an important backdrop to an examination of the role of race, culture, and national origin in adoption. They help to illustrate the complexities posed by the array of factors that have influenced adoption in racial, cultural, and national origin terms and that have presented challenges to mutual understanding in an area in which individual, family, group, community, and societal interests and values come into play.

A Brief Historical Context

The role of race, culture, and national origin in contemporary adoption is grounded, to some degree, in the history of adoption practice, policy, and law in this country. Although the historical antecedents of these issues will be reviewed in greater detail in each of the sections that follow, a brief synthesis of the history of adoption in relation to these issues is presented here. Since the

1800s, adoption has existed in some recognizable form in the United States. Most states, beginning with Massachusetts, enacted legislation governing adoption in the second half of the 19th century [Cole & Donley 1990], laws that addressed various aspects of adoption but did not explicitly focus on issues related to race, culture, and national origin. Society itself, however, provided the norms with regard to racial and cultural issues in the form of a strong social preference for keeping children within their own racial and ethnic communities. In the 19th and early 20th century, the children who were placed for adoption were, by and large, Caucasian children, and the issue was primarily one of sustaining the religious affiliation of children by placing them with adoptive families of the same religion as the child's birth family [Hewins & Webster 1927]. Religious "matching," in effect, ensured cultural matching of children and adoptive families.

In contrast to the current controversies related to racial and cultural "matching" in adoption, the earlier controversies centered on religion. The political and social power of the religious "matching" issue in the mid-1800s is illustrated by the extent to which religion became intertwined with the efforts of Charles Loring Brace to permanently place large numbers of street children in New York City with new families in the Midwest and South. Brace's "orphan trains," which began operating in the 1850s and continued through the 1920s, drew significant criticism from Catholics who suspected that Brace and his organization, the Children's Aid Society, were proselytizing and attempting to convert Catholic children to Protestantism [Langsam 1964; Cole & Donley 1990]. L. Silliman Ives, a prominent Catholic in New York City, for example, publicly renounced the perceived Protestant bias of the Society and claimed that the orphan train movement was designed to sever Catholic children's ties with their own faith [Langsam 1964]. Efforts were made to establish an alternative "society" to place Catholic children with Catholic families, but it proved to be unsuccessful as many Catholic families in the New York City area were recent immigrants and not yet sufficiently established to take responsibility for additional children. The

feeling that Catholic children should sustain their religious connection was so strong that, rather than risk losing children to
Protestant families, most Catholic children were placed in indus-
trial schools or in institutional care rather than placed for adoption [Langsam 1964].

The importance of religious "matching" persisted in adoption
throughout the first half of the 20th century [Cole and Donley
1990], and was even further strengthened by the evolving philoso-
phy, which took full form in the 1950s, that adoptive families and
children should be "the same" in virtually every aspect. At that
juncture, criteria for matching children with adoptive families
explicitly came to include not only the same religious affiliation
of adoptive family and birth parents but, importantly, close
physical resemblance, including likeness in race, cultural background, and national identity [Gill, in press]. The goal was to
create, as closely as possible, the family that the adopted child
would have had if her birth parents had been able to raise her [Gill,
in press].

The desirability of racial and cultural matching of children
and adoptive families in the 1950s and the 1960s was consistent
with the social and political forces of the time that viewed "racial
mixing," in particular, as unacceptable. Well into the 1960s, many
states outlawed miscegenation (the marriage of a black person to
a white person) and made interracial adoption illegal [Pohl &
Harris 1992]. Racial "matching" of children and adoptive families,
as a result, existed within a social climate that essentially supported sameness [Gill, in press]. There were, however, acceptable
exceptions to this prevailing norm. Transracial adoptions were
considered appropriate for the small number of children adopted
internationally from Asia following the involvement of the United
States in World War II, the Korean War, and later the Vietnam War.
Similarly, as discussed later, the placement of American Indian
children with non-Indian families constituted acceptable "non-
matching." In the late 1960s, with the advent of the civil rights
movement, there was a significant shift in the overall social
climate, marking the beginning of a re-evaluation of the role of race

and culture in adoption. The effects of this shift on children of color in the United States and in relation to a broader practice of international adoption will be discussed in the following sections of this book.

Part I

Foster Care and Adoption: The Role of Race and Culture

The role of race and culture in adoption has come to be a principal issue in the policy debates related to permanency outcomes for children in foster care in this country. The practice of transracial adoption in particular has become an overarching issue that, in some minds, has contributed to and, in other minds, obscured an understanding of the fundamental problems that have led to disproportionately large numbers of children of color in foster care and a growth in the number of children of color in care—particularly African American children—waiting for adoptive families [Courtney 1997].

Transracial adoption—despite the popular viewpoint that it represents the "solution" to the backlog of waiting children of color in care [Pierce 1998]—offers an approach that may affect, in reality, only a small number of children in foster care [Perry 1990/ 1991]. More realistically, as a policy and practice issue, it provides a prism through which broader questions related to the role of race and culture in permanency planning in general and in adoption in particular may be examined. In this part of this book, transracial adoption and the controversy surrounding it will be used as the touchstone for a consideration of broader issues related to the role of race and culture in the adoption of children in foster care. The primary focus will be on African American children in the foster care system, although the role of race and culture as they relate to Latino and other children of color in foster care will be referenced to the extent that research and literature provide guidance. In the following section of this book, the role of race and culture in the adoption of American Indian children will be considered separately as this issue presents unique historical, legal, and practice considerations.

9

The Policy and Practice Environment: Transracial Adoption as the Galvanizing Issue

Adoption itself has become more of a permanency option "of choice" for children in the foster care system over the last several years. In the 1980 Adoption Assistance and Child Welfare Act (P.L. 96-272), adoption was listed as the second permanency alternative—the option to be considered when children could not or would not be reunited with their birth families. Although adoption lost favor as a permanency option for children in care in the early 1990s as family preservation and family reunification became the prevailing policy and practice goals, adoption was revalidated as a "preferred" option with the 1997 passage of the Adoption and Safe Families Act (P.L. 105-89). Coinciding with these legislative developments, the passage of the Multi-Ethnic Placement Act in 1994 (P.L. 103-382) and the Interethnic Placement Act amendments in 1996 (P.L. 104-188) catapulted transracial adoption into a prominent position in terms of both policy and practice, giving rise to vigorous debate about the practice itself and more broadly the extent to which race and culture should or should not matter in adoptive family formation.

The forces that prompted the passage of the Multi-Ethnic Placement Act and later the Interethnic Placement Act amendments [collectively "MEPA"] ultimately succeeded in disallowing the consideration of race in making adoption decisions for children in foster care. Initially, the 1994 Act—which prohibited agencies from delaying or denying an adoptive placement on the basis of race, color, or national origin—nevertheless allowed consideration, as "one of a number of factors" in determining a child's adoptive placement, the child's race and the prospective adoptive parents' ability to meet the needs of a child of a particular racial or cultural background. The 1996 amendments, however, eliminated consideration of race and prohibited agencies from taking the child's or the prospective adoptive parents' race, color, or national origin into account in making an adoptive placement. Noncompliance with this mandate is penalized with a significant reduction in federal child welfare funds. MEPA, at minimum, translated into law the belief that race and, by extension, culture are irrelevant in adoption; the penalty provisions suggest that it may have gone further and incorporated a belief that not only are race and culture irrelevant, but a focus on these factors in adoption is sufficiently harmful at some level as to justify "punishment." As the controversy regarding transracial adoption clearly indicates, there is within the adoption community widespread disagreement with these underlying beliefs and a strong competing position that race and culture do indeed matter in adoption.

The Conflicting Perspectives

As Courtney [1997, p. 750] has noted, the debate on the issue of race and culture in adoption has been intense with "scant middle ground." It has been wide-ranging, with arguments made at a number of levels, reflecting the complexity of issues related to race and culture in U.S. society generally, and in the context of adoptive family formation in particular. At one level, the debate on the role of race and culture, particularly as it has surfaced in the context of transracial adoption, has been cast in broad sociocultural terms—with arguments made, on the one hand, that transracial adoption—by rendering race and culture irrelevant—is a "blatant form of race and cultural genocide" [Merritt 1985] to assertions, on the other hand, either that transracial adoption provides the means to remove children from a harmful "subculture" and give them access to "mainstream American culture and language" [Kramer 1994, p. 23] or that transracial adoption is consistent with the values of a "colorblind" society [Kennedy 1994].

Perry [1993/1994, p. 38] characterizes the current debate as reflective of two distinct perspectives: "liberal colorblind individualism" and "color and community consciousness." These perspectives, representing two distinct views of the fundamental role of race in U.S. society, diverge on three key points. First, colorblind individualism sees the eradication of racism as achievable; color and community consciousness, by contrast, views racism as both a pervasive and permanent part of U.S. society. Second, colorblind individualism champions the ideal of complete elimination of any consideration of race; color and community consciousness embraces multiculturalism and places value on sustaining cultural diversity within U.S. society. Third, colorblind individualism places the individual at the center of any analysis of rights and interests; color and community consciousness places an equivalent emphasis on the rights and interests of individuals and of the groups to which individuals belong [Perry 1993/1994, p. 43].

These perspectives, as developed by Perry [1993/1994], lead to very different assessments of the role of race and culture in adoption. At the "rights" level, colorblind individualism focuses on the adult who is accorded the "right" to make decisions regarding the way in which he or she will form a family without the interference of the state. By contrast, color and community consciousness, particularly in relation to the African American community, emphasizes "rights" in relation to the struggles of the community to autonomously establish and sustain family life in an environment that often has been hostile to the community's interests. With regard to the role of race in parent-child relationships, colorblind individualism maintains that racial differences between parent and child are not important, while color and community consciousness demands that such differences be acknowledged and addressed because the child's racial identity is of critical importance. Finally, the two perspectives view children's interests in radically different ways. Colorblind individualism assumes that the best interests of the child are served by a focus on an immediate adoptive placement without regard to the race of the adoptive family and without consideration of any community interests associated with the child's adoption. By contrast, color and community consciousness focuses on the child's interests in the context of her link to and identification with her racial/cultural community [Perry 1993/1994, p. 53].

Colorblindness—the view of race as an irrelevant factor in the adoption of children of color—is a concept that has shaped the work of several legal scholars who promote transracial adoption [Banks 1998; Bartholet 1991; Howard 1984; Kennedy 1998; Mahoney 1991]. Themes related to achieving a nonracist society and the importance of meeting the immediate placement interests of individual children to the exclusion of any group or community interests characterize the writings of these academics. Kennedy [1998], for example, explicitly endorses the value of "colorblindness," asserting that race should not play any role in the adoption of children of color. He informed a Congressional committee studying interethnic adoptions that:

> Race matching ... harms the entire society morally and spiritually by reiterating the baneful notion, long entrenched in law and custom, that people of different races should not be permitted to disregard racial distinctions when creating families. A preference—any preference— for same race adoptions or foster care stigmatizes interracial child placements as second-rate alternatives, the arrangement authorities turn to when other, "better" possibilities are foreclosed. A preference for same-race placements buttresses the notion that in social affairs race matters and should matter in some fundamental, unbridgeable, permanent sense.

Although "best interest of the child" often appears as a underpinning for the colorblind individualism approach advanced by these writers, aspects of this perspective, as articulated by some transracial adoption proponents, suggest that adult interests, particularly in relation to autonomy in forming their families as they choose, may be an equal if not more compelling force than the interests of children. Bartholet's analysis of the harmfulness of "race matching" policies [1991], for example, appears to place great emphasis on rights of adults to create a multiracial family if they so choose. Perry [1993/1994] strongly criticizes this approach and argues that the individual rights and interests asserted by Bartholet and others may have less to do with autonomy in family formation and more to do with maintaining decision-making power within the majority culture. As has been pointed out by a number of writers [Billingsley & Giovanni 1972; Chestang 1983; Lum 1986; Mindel & Habenstein 1981; Montiel & Wong 1983; Smith & Stewart 1973; Walters 1982], race relations in the

U.S. historically have been characterized by the exercise of power by Caucasians in matters bearing on African Americans and other people of color.

The National Association of Black Social Workers (NABSW), generally identified as the most vocal opponent of transracial adoption, perhaps has articulated most clearly the "color and community consciousness" perspective described by Perry. The NABSW first stated its opposition to transracial adoption in 1972, taking the position that African American children physically, emotionally, and culturally belong in African American families [National Association of Black Social Workers 1972]. The NABSW's concerns about transracial adoption were reiterated in 1985 when the president of NABSW, William Merritt [1985], testified before Congress:

> We are opposed to transracial adoptions as a solution to the permanent placement of Black children. We have an ethical, moral, and professional obligation to oppose transracial adoption. We are therefore legally justified in our efforts to protect the rights of Black children, Black families, and the Black community. We view the placement of Black children in white homes as a hostile act against our community. It is a blatant form of racial and cultural genocide.

Subsequently, in 1994, the NABSW issued a position statement somewhat modifying its position but maintaining a focus on the role of the African American community. In *Preserving African-American Families*, the NASBW emphasized the need to preserve families through reunification or adoption of children by biological relatives; identified adoption by a family of the child's own race as a "secondary priority;" and recognized the appropriateness of transracial adoption only "after documented evidence of unsuccessful same race placement has been reviewed and supported by appropriate representation of the African American community" [1994, p. 4].

The color and community consciousness perspective takes a broad view of the best interests of a child by linking the child's needs with the interests of the child's racial and cultural community. This perspective highlights, in addition to the interests of the individual child, issues related to group preservation—the maintenance of the integrity of the community in the face of demographic threats posed by the loss of children who, because they are adopted transracially, fail to identify with the community. Howe [1997, p. 417], for example, writes:

> By according no legitimacy to the group interests of African Americans and focusing just on the individual rights of African American children, these legal champions [of transracial adoption] assure a supply of children to meet the market demands of white adults seeking to parent whatever children they select. These actions rob African-Americans of the privilege and responsibility of caring for their own children. No group can be assured continued existence and vitality if it does not bear and rear its own children.

Perry [1993/1994] acknowledges that there may be disagreement regarding the extent to which the individual interests of children and community interests should be linked together. She argues, however, that from the perspective of color and community consciousness, group interests cannot be wholly discounted. She writes that, at minimum, "Black children should not be treated as if they come from no community or from a cultural tradition without value" [1993/1994, p. 67].

These broad perspectives have infused the policy debate regarding the "best interests" of children of color in foster care and, specifically, how permanency is best promoted for the growing number of children of color in care who will not be reunited with their birth families. In this context, transracial adoption has been promoted as maximizing the "best interests" of children of color in foster care by providing them with the permanency of family which, it is asserted, they would not otherwise realized [Silverman 1993]. This position, consistent with Perry's description of the colorblind individualism perspective, seeks support in studies that have found that children who are transracially adopted fare as well as in-race adopted children—studies that typically report outcomes for children adopted transracially as infants and not as older children in foster care [Silverman 1993].

The other side of the debate, consistent with Perry's description of the color and community consciousness perspective, is that transracial adoption works against the "best interests" of children in care because it carries with it the significant risk, if not certainty, that children of color will lose their sense of racial identity [Chestang 1972; Chimezie 1975; National Association of Black Social Workers 1994; Small 1984]. This position focuses on potential problems for the transracially-adopted child in dealing with the majority culture and identifying with his or her minority culture, and relies on research showing that transracially adopted children experience problems with racial identity [Andujo 1988; McRoy & Zurcher 1983]. This position is consistent with the body of psychology and child development literature that has emphasized the relationship between ego identity and self- esteem on the one hand, and racial identity on the other [Erickson 1968; Logan 1981; Chestang 1984], and that has focused on the development of a healthy racial identity and "parental nurturing ... [to] offset the effects of an antagonistic society" [Comer & Poussaint 1975, p. 110].

Research on Transracial Adoption

Perhaps in no other area of child welfare has the meaningfulness of research findings been so debated as in the area of transracial adoption—findings that offer conflicting views of the role of race and culture in adoption and the extent to which children's "best interests" are or are not promoted by taking race and culture into account. The current body of research on outcomes associated with transracial adoption has primarily focused on the adoption of African American children by Caucasian parents, the aspect of transracial adoption that has generated the greatest controversy [Courtney 1997]. In general, studies demonstrate no significant differences between children adopted in-racially and transracially with regard to overall well-being [Fanshel 1972; Feigelman & Silverman 1983, 1984; Bagley 1993b; Barth & Berry 1988; Shireman & Johnson 1988; Simon et al. 1994; Vroegh 1997; Feigelman 1998; Brooks & Barth 1999]. The research is not entirely uniform, however, as some studies have found that African American and Latino children who are transracially adopted exhibit some level of conflict related to racial identity [McRoy & Zurcher 1983; Andujo 1988] and African American transracial adoptees prefer to have Caucasian friends [McRoy & Zurcher 1983; Simon et al. 1994]. Other studies suggest that transracial adoptees may experience certain "adoptive stressors" that have a negative effect on psychological adjustment [DeBerry et al.1996]. Because the findings suggest both positive and negative outcomes associated with transracial adoption, the research has been utilized to support the proposition that race and culture are essentially irrelevant to the well-being of adopted children and to support the proposition that race and culture do indeed matter in terms of personal identity and social relationships.

It has been consistently pointed out that the major research in the area of transracial adoption is undermined by deficits in the methodological rigor of the studies that have been conducted [Courtney 1997; Brooks et al. 1997; Rushton & Minnis 1997; Alexander & Curtis 1996; Goddard 1996; Taylor & Thornton 1996; Harrison 1996; Willis 1996; Grotevant 1988]. The generalizability of the findings is compromised by small sample sizes that make it impossible to rule out almost any effect of transracial adoption; reliance on "convenience" samples of volunteers who are not necessarily representative of the population of transracial adopters or adoptees; reliance on parental reports of children's feelings and reactions in assessing outcomes rather than direct reports from adoptees as children, adolescents, or adults; the focus of these studies on children adopted as infants rather than children adopted at older ages from foster care; and the failure to take into account significant attrition in sample size over time that may lead to biased results. Courtney [1997, p. 753] has concluded that "strictly speaking, empirical research has not yet 'proven' transracial adoption to be good or bad for children" and is unlikely to do so in the future, with the result that:

> [T]hose with strongly held views are likely to maintain their convictions: advocates of transracial adoption will continue to believe that the research supports their beliefs, while opponents will contend that transracial adoption is harmful or that the jury is still out.

Key Issues Related to the Role of Race and Culture in Adoption for Children of Color in Foster Care

An understanding of the role that race and culture should play in adoption may, ultimately, rest on clearly articulated values applied in a framework that is informed by the existing data, research, and practice-based knowledge. In the following section, some of the key issues that affect adoption planning and services for children of color in foster care in the United States are considered, and the current research and the practice-based literature that address these issues are reviewed. This analysis is offered in an effort to promote a fuller understanding of the complex racial and cultural issues that are intertwined with adoption planning and services for the growing population of children of color in foster care and to provide a framework for considering the values that should underlie policy and practice in this area in the future.

A review of the research and literature on issues bearing on race and culture in adoption suggests that in the context of permanency planning for children of color in foster care, there are four key issue areas warranting review and analysis. The first area relates to the "best interests" of children of color in the foster care system who wait for adoptive families and the realities associated with the availability of Caucasian families as adoptive resources for this growing population of children. The second area is that of kinship care—the care of children in foster care by relatives—and the extent to which this form of care, which implicitly raises considerations related to race and culture, informs an understanding of the permanency needs of children of color. The third area is that of the adoption of children of color by families of color who are not related to them but who are recruited as adoptive resources, and the extent to which these family resources have been effectively reached by child welfare systems. The fourth area relates to the needs of children already placed with foster parents of a race and culture other their own—with issues related to permanency planning in the face of potentially competing interests, including race- and culture-based needs.

The "Best Interests" of Children of Color and the Availability of Caucasian Families as Adoptive Resources

The enormity of the challenges related to permanency planning for children of color in foster care is well documented. Data establish that children of color comprise a substantial and disproportionate percentage of children in the foster care system. As of March 31, 1999, when there were an estimated 547,000 children in foster care, 43% of the children were African American and 15% were Latino [U.S. Department of Health and Human Services 2000]. Data from individual jurisdictions across the United States indicate that the percentage of children in care who are from minority communities is even higher. The Chapin Hall Center for Children at the University of Chicago [1997], for example, found that the percentage of children in foster care in Illinois who were African American increased from approximately 58% in 1988 to 70% in 1994. In California, the percentage of children in foster care who were Latino rose over that same time period from approximately 20% to more than 30% [Chapin Hall 1997]. These figures are particularly dramatic considering the ethnicity of the child population in the United States: in 1997, Caucasian/Non-Hispanic children constituted 66%, African American children 15%, and Latino children 15% of the total U.S. child population [U.S. Bureau of the Census 1998].

Once in foster care, African American children and Latino children remain in care for longer periods of time than do Caucasian children [Goerge et al. 1995]. A recent study of children placed in foster care in New York City for the first time in 1992, for example, found that one-quarter of African American children were still in care as of January 1998 as compared to one-fifth of the Latino children and one-tenth of the Caucasian children [Child Welfare Watch 1998]. Similarly, a study of length of stay for children of color in Washington State found that 20% of African American children and 22% of American Indian children remained in foster care for more than four years compared to 12% of Caucasian children [English & Clark 1996].

Children of color are also overrepresented among children in foster care who are awaiting adoptive families. At the end of FY1990, 43% of the children in public child welfare agency care who were awaiting adoption were African American and approximately 7% were Latino [Tatara 1993]. As of March 31, 1999, of the 117,000 children in need of adoption planning and services, 51% were African American and 11% were Latino [U.S. Department of Health and Human Services 2000]. Data indicate that in some major urban areas, such as New York City and Detroit, African American children comprise approximately 80% of the children needing adoptive families [McKenzie 1993; Jones 1992]. Research also suggests that children of color in foster care are less likely to ever be adopted. Barth [1997] found that African American children were more than twice as likely to remain in foster care as to be adopted; Caucasian children were about twice as likely to be adopted as to remain in foster care; and Latino children were about equally likely to remain in foster care as to be adopted.

These data suggest that race and culture are significant factors associated with the entry of children into foster care, the length of time they remain in care pending the determination of a permanency plan, the length of their wait for adoptive families once it is determined that they will not be reunited with their birth families, and the probability that they will be adopted. There appears to be little dispute regarding the role of race and culture in relation to these aspects of the experiences of children of color as they move through the child welfare system [Kellogg Foundation n.d.]. On the other hand, there has been disagreement on the extent to which race and culture should be factors in decision-making related to children exiting foster care through adoption.

On the one hand, there are those who maintain that the reason that children of color remain in foster care for extended periods of time and are not readily placed with adoptive families is that agencies have firmly adhered to policies that require a racial or cultural "match" between child and adoptive family. These writers maintain that barriers to transracial adoption have posed an important, if not the major, obstacle to permanency for children of color in foster care. Simon and associates [1994, p. 116], for example, have contended that abolition of "same race" adoption placement practice and broad use of transracial adoption would move "thousands of children who are available for adoption out of the institutions and out of temporary placements and into permanent homes." Bartholet [1993, p. 99], likewise, maintains that "very large numbers of black children in need of homes are spending significant amounts of their childhoods in foster and institutional care rather than permanent adoptive homes because of policies against transracial placement." Inherent in these assertions are assumptions that large numbers of Caucasian families stand ready to adopt children of color in foster care and that what stands between children and adoptive families is "same race" placement criteria. Both of these assumptions, which serve as the basis for current transracial adoption policies, warrant examination.

Assumption # 1: Large numbers of Caucasian families stand ready to adopt children of color in foster care. The extent to which Caucasian families desire to adopt children of color must be considered in light of the demographics of adoption in two very different contexts—infant adoption and foster care adoption. From the perspective of "demand" for adoption, it is clear that the number of individuals seeking to adopt is increasing. Data indicate that in 1988, about 200,000 women were actively seeking at any point in time to adopt a child [Bachrach et al. 1991] and that by 1996, the number had risen to approximately 500,000 [National Center for Health Statistics 1997]. Women who seek to adopt are predominantly Caucasian women who pursue adoption because of infertility [Bachrach et al. 1991]. With the exception of a very small percentage of these women, prospective adopters seek to adopt healthy white infants or toddlers [see Bachrach et al. 1991; Courtney 1997].

From the perspective of meeting the adoption interests of a population of predominantly Caucasian women, the key demographic is the number of healthy white infants available for adoption. Historically, Caucasian women rather than women from other racial/ethnic groups have placed their infants for adoption [Mosher & Bachrach 1996]. The rate at which never-married Caucasian women place their newborns for adoption, however, has declined—decreasing from 19% of all births in 1965–1972 to 3% of those births in 1982–1988 [Bachrach et al. 1992] and even more—to a rate of only 1.7% in the first half of 1990 [Chandra et al. 1999]. Among never-married African American and Latina women, the adoption placement rate has always been low—well below 2% of all births [Chandra et al. 1999; Mosher & Bachrach 1996].

With the significantly diminished rate of placement of Caucasian infants for adoption, the number of these children available for adoption has not met the increased demand for adoption on the part of Caucasian women. Interest among Caucasian adopters may have turned to international adoption (discussed later), and, to some statistically undetermined degree, to African American infants in this country [Howard 1984]. Bartholet [1993, p. 113], for example, states:

> You have only to step into the world of adoption to realize that it is largely peopled by prospective adoptive parents in search of white children.... Many white adopters start the adoption process with no apparent racial preferences. Many others begin their quest thinking of a white child and turn to transracial adoption after considering their options. For them, transracial adoption may appear to be a second choice. But the fact is that for a very large number of adoptive parents, adoption itself is a second choice, forced upon them by their inability to reproduce.

To the extent that this observation reflects the reality of current efforts in pursuit of infant adoption [see Chandra et al.

1999], it raises a number of issues, not the least of which is the question of the weight that should be placed on the interests of adults who seek to adopt children of certain races—an issue quite distinct from the principle of "best interests of the child" but one that has been raised consistently in the context of the debate about transracial adoption. Should opportunities to adopt children of color transracially be viewed from the perspective of adults' desires to adopt, with emphasis on broadly making available to Caucasian adopters children of different races and cultures? Should adopters' stated desires to adopt transracially be entitled to deference?

Adoption practice has recognized that prospective adoptive parents are entitled to decline consideration of children of certain races for adoption. Although Banks [1998, p. 875] promotes a "blanket prohibition on the expression of racial preferences" by adoptive parents with regard to the children they will adopt, most proponents of transracial adoption who have addressed this issue have endorsed the principle that prospective adopters have the right to specify the race of the children whom they will adopt [Bartholet 1991; Mahoney 1991]. In practice, this prerogative— generally based on a recognition of adults' autonomy interests in making decisions as to how they will form their families—has manifested itself primarily in adults' desires to adopt children of their own race and a desire to not be considered as adoptive parents for children of other races. As the demographics of adoption have changed, however, this prerogative may itself have shifted to suggest that prospective adoptive parents, having come to terms with the fact that an infant of their own race may not be readily available for adoption, should be able to adopt an infant of their "second choice" race or culture. Some have contended that to deprive Caucasian adults of the right to adopt children of color is akin to "reverse discrimination" in the employment or higher education context [Hayes 1993, 1995]—where courts have held that race may not be taken into account with regard to "scarce resources" such as jobs or medical school admission. Whether the scarcity of white infants available for adoption gives rise to a "right" to adopt infants of color raises a significant ethical issue. This issue may be further complicated by recent interpretations of

MEPA indicating that although adoptive parents retain the right to specify the race of the child whom they will adopt, a birth parent's preference regarding the race of the adoptive parent(s) for her child is not entitled to deference [Pollack 1998].

It has become clear that as the supply of Caucasian infants has decreased and the willingness of Caucasian adopters to consider the adoption of African American infants has increased to some level [see Chandra et al. 1999], a number of agencies have moved toward transracial adoptive placements. Beginning in the 1970s with the decline in the number of relinquishments of Caucasian newborns, some adoption agencies that previously had not served African American women or accepted relinquishments of African American infants expanded their services to include these infants [McRoy 1989]. A 1990–1991 national survey of 87 adoption agencies in 25 states found that traditional private adoption agencies were placing almost one-half of their African American children, the vast majority of whom were infants, transracially [Gilles & Kroll 1991]. The ability of Caucasian adopters to pay the fees of private agencies placing infants for adoption and the dependence of agencies on income from fees also have been cited as factors influencing this change in practice [Austin 1988; Howe 1997; McRoy 1989].

The demographics of "demand" and "supply" in the arena of foster care and adoption—the primary context for the transracial adoption policy debate because of the applicability of MEPA to publicly funded agencies—however, are far different than those of infant adoption. With regard to adult demand for adoption, the research and literature suggest far less interest on the part of Caucasian adopters in older children of color, particularly children with histories of abuse and neglect and foster care placement. Studies that specifically examine parental preferences related to race, disability status, and age are somewhat dated but tend to suggest that adoptive families in general do not express an interest in adopting older children, children with disabilities, or children of African American heritage [Meezan et al. 1978; Kossoudji 1989]. While it is possible that attitudes among prospective adopters have changed, neither the research nor recent statistics suggest a greater demand by Caucasian families for African American children in general nor for older children [Courtney 1997].

The demographics of children served through foster care and adoption raise questions about the extent to which the actual adoption interests of Caucasians are directed toward children in foster care in general or children of color in foster care in particular. Data clearly demonstrates that children waiting in foster care for adoptive families are not the healthy infants desired by the would-be adopters described by Bartholet and others. Data from the Multistate Foster Care Data Archive [Goerge et al. 1994, 1995] indicate that the majority of children in care, including children of color, are not infants but older children. Data from the U.S. Department of Health and Human Services (HHS) [2000] indicate that children in foster care waiting for adoption have a mean age of 8 years and a median age of 7.7 years. Almost two-thirds of the children waiting for adoptive families are 6 years or older [HHS 2000].

Other data show that the health of these children often has been compromised by a variety of factors, including histories of abuse and neglect and multiple placements after children enter foster care. There has been a steady increase in the percentage of children in foster care with "special needs"—which include physical, mental health, and developmental problems—awaiting adoptive placements, rising from 47.4% in FY1984 to 71.7% in FY1990 [Tatara 1993] to 86% in FY1998 (HHS 2000]. A recent survey of 25 states by the Child Welfare League of America [1997] found that 93% of the children placed for adoption in 1996 had special needs. Studies also suggest that growing numbers of children entering care have significant health problems or are at risk of physical or developmental problems because of prenatal substance exposure [U.S. General Accounting Office 1994]. These age and health characteristics of children in foster care who are freed for adoption, a large percentage of whom are African American, suggest that these children are not the children sought by the great majority of prospective Caucasian adoptive parents. The National Association of Black Social Workers [1994] has estimated that only 1% or less of Caucasian families expressing an interest in adopting African American children requested older children (over the age of eight years), sibling groups, or children with physical or emotional disabilities. Similarly, Courtney [1997, p. 760] has observed:

> Although thousands of African American children and other children of color spend long periods of time in out-of-home care, very few of them exhibit the qualities necessary to move them to the top of the preference lists of the relatively small proportion of potential Caucasian adopters who appear willing to adopt children of color. This appears to be particularly true for African American children in out of home care.

It is difficult to make a strong case that policies promoting transracial adoption respond to a significant level of interest among prospective Caucasian adopters in general in adopting children of color—and particularly African American children—in foster care, other than in a largely theoretical sense. While transracial adoption may hypothetically "open the field" to prospective Caucasian adopters, the "field" based on adult preferences appears to be infant adoption and not the waiting population of children of color in foster care. Some critics of transracial adoption have highlighted this likelihood, noting that the actual interest of adopters, "a steady supply of infants to satisfy a demand," is being hidden "under a halo of professed concern for the well-being of African-American children in foster care" [Howe 1997, p. 423].

Assumption # 2: Practices related to "matching" children and adoptive families on race and culture prevent the adoption of children of color in foster care. Underlying this assumption is the belief that a large number of children of color will not have the benefit of permanency in their lives unless "race-matching" policies are entirely prohibited and transracial adoption is widely promoted and practiced. From this perspective, transracial adoption is seen as an optimal solution for ensuring permanency for children of color in care whose adoptive placements have purportedly been delayed or denied because of "race matching" policies.

This assumption suffers from a reliance on the underlying assumption just discussed that large numbers of Caucasian families stand ready to adopt children of color in foster care. As the analysis of the interests of Caucasians in adopting children of color in foster care suggests, there may be a very limited supply of traditional Caucasian adopters who will step forward to adopt these children irrespective of transracial adoption policies. Courtney [1997, p. 771], for example, contends that "[T]he naive notion that thousands of children taken from impoverished parents will all be magically swooped up by loving adoptive families" is a "cruel delusion" that fails to take into account the realities of the demographic dynamics of adoption and the public child welfare system.

Nevertheless, there has been a tendency to rely on data reflecting low rates of transracial adoption and an interpretation of such data as providing evidence of "race-based" barriers to permanency planning for children of color in foster care [see Nadel 1998]. There is no definitive source of data on a national basis regarding the current number of children of color in foster care who are adopted transracially. Preliminary federal data for FY1999, however, suggests that very low percentages of Caucasian children in foster care are placed with at least one parent who is of a different race or ethnicity as the child (4% of Caucasian children placed with married couples and 1% of Caucasian children placed with single females) and that higher percentages of minority children are placed with at least one parent of a different race or ethnicity (25% of minority children placed with married couples and 12% of minority children placed with single females) [Maza 2000]. A Child Welfare League of America [1995] survey of 22 states, for example, found that 4% of all adoptions in 1993 were transracial, and Stolley [1993] reported that only about 1% of all adoptions involved adoptions of African American children by white parents. Avery and Mont [1994], in their New York State study, found that approximately 11% of adoptions among a sample of 258 families were transracial. The researchers found that in most instances, Caucasian parents adopted African American children [10.68%] and only in a very small number of adoptions [.83% or 3 cases] did African American parents adopt a Caucasian child [Avery & Mont 1994].

Even if these studies regarding the incidence of transracial adoption provided reliable indicators of the transracial adoption rate, they do not offer support for the proposition that greater use of transracial adoption would enhance permanency for children of color in foster care. If a larger percentage of all adoptions of children in care were transracial as opposed to in-race, would that data suggest enhanced permanency for children? Would higher rates of transracial adoption, as opposed to the realization of other permanency options, translate into a more timely permanency for children in foster care? Neither the data nor the literature supports an affirmative answer to either question. The meaningfulness of transracial adoption rates have, in fact, been questioned even as to the extent to which they reflect the level of state compliance with MEPA mandates. Nadel [1998], in the General Accounting Office study of state implementation of MEPA, cautioned that there are inherent difficulties in interpreting changes in the percentages of same-race as opposed to transracial adoption. A low percentage of transracial adoption could indicate agencies' failure to consider Caucasian families as adoptive resources for children of color or could indicate agencies' successful recruitment of larger numbers of adoptive parents of color [Nadel 1998].

Data regarding the adoption of Caucasian children in foster care, however, do appear to undermine a reliance on "racial barriers" as the explanation for the difficulties in placing children in foster care with adoptive families. The most recent national data indicate that 32% of waiting children in foster care are Caucasian [HHS 2000], a population of children who theoretically should not be waiting in care if "same race" placement practice were in force and large numbers of Caucasian families stood ready to adopt children in foster care. Data from the Children's Services Archive at the University of California, Berkeley, similarly show that even given the assumed demand for Caucasian infants, 16% of the Caucasian infants who entered foster care and who were placed with nonrelated foster parents were still in care four years later [Courtney 1997]. Although the data does not reflect how many of these infants had the goal of adoption, the combination of young age at entry, placement with nonkin foster parents, and length of time of care (indicating difficulties with family reunification) suggest that adoption was likely the plan for a significant number of these children [Courtney 1997]. Adoptive placements, however, were not achieved after four years in foster care despite these children's desirable qualities of age and race at the time of entry into care [see Barth 1997].

There are no systematic studies that demonstrate that policies or practices favoring the adoptive placement of African American children with African American families have been responsible for extended delays in placing these children with adoptive families [Perry 1993/1994]. The literature instead strongly suggests that factors other than racial barriers present powerful obstacles to adoption for children of color. McRoy and colleagues [1997, p. 100-101] write that the growing number of older children of color in foster care is the result not of "policies promoting same-race placement" but of such factors as "the disproportionately high number of African American children being removed from their biological families, the delays in termination of parental rights, the inequities in length of stay in out-of-home care, and the obstacles to African American adoptions."

Data clearly support these authors' identification of the disproportionate removal of African American children from their families and placement in foster care [Tatara 1993; HHS 2000] and the inequitable length of time that African American children remain in care [Goerge et al. 1995]. The nature and scope of child welfare interventions and services to families of color consistently have been found to fall short of those provided to Caucasian families [Courtney et al. 1996; Billingsley & Giovannoni 1972; Hogan & Siu 1988], suggesting a service base that has not promoted timely permanency planning for these children and families. Preventive and supportive child welfare services have only recently been offered to families of color [Billingsley & Giovannoni 1972; Hogan & Siu 1988], and to the extent that preventive services are offered, they tend to be at a far less intensive level than the services offered to Caucasians families [Courtney et al. 1996].

At the intervention service level, African American children and families are disproportionately represented among families subject to investigations for child abuse and neglect [McRoy et al. 1997], and African American children enter foster care at higher rates than Caucasian children. Morton [1993], for example, found in one state that, compared to 1 in 100 Caucasian infants coming into care, 1 in 20 African American infants born in the year under study entered foster care. Once in foster care, African American children are likely to remain longer, to receive fewer services, and to visit with their parents less often than is the case for Caucasian children [Close 1983; Stehno 1990]. Problems related to permanency planning, including delays in termination of parental rights, have been criticized for delaying adoption for all children in foster care, including children of color. The General Accounting Office [Kusserow 1991], for example, found substantial deficiencies in child welfare practice in relation to achievement of permanency for children in care, including failures to engage in permanency planning for children from the time they enter care; deficiencies in the legal and judicial systems, including delays in scheduling hearings and inadequate legal representation of parents and children; and limitations on needed resources in both the child welfare and legal/judicial systems to effect timely permanency plans for children in foster care through reunification or adoption. It was concerns about these systemic issues that led to the enactment of the Adoption and Safe Families Act of 1997 (P.L. 105-89) and prompted other federal legislative efforts to streamline the judicial processes involved in permanency planning [see Model Children's Court Advisory Committee 1998]. The impact of these identified deficiencies on the population of children of color has been particularly significant because of their disproportionate representation in the foster care system generally and, more specifically, among children waiting for adoptive families.

The many factors affecting the disproportionate representation of children of color in foster care raise questions regarding the extent to which these children's extended stays in care can be attributed to adoption placement practices that emphasize children's racial and cultural identities and needs. They also suggest that from a systems perspective, practices that render race and culture irrelevant in adoption planning and services are unlikely to lead to significantly improved permanency outcomes through adoption for children of color, the purported goal of transracial adoption practice and policy. The range of complex issues that have placed substantial barriers to permanency for children of color in foster care, combined with the realities associated with the current supply of adoptive family resources for children, suggest that a narrow definition of the problem in "same race placement" terms fails to appreciate the nature and scope of the problem. At the same time, the emphasis on transracial adoption and the diminishment of the value of race and culture may seriously and harmfully underestimate the important psychological needs of children of color, as discussed later.

Kinship Foster Care and the Role of Race and Color in Permanency Planning for Children in Foster Care

Those who make assumptions about the role of "race-based" criteria in preventing or delaying adoption for children of color in foster care have generally paid little attention to kinship care—a factor increasingly associated with permanency for children of color. There has been a dramatic growth over the past decade in kinship care—in which children are placed by child welfare agencies with relatives when they must be removed from the custody of their parents (generally referred to as "formal kinship care") as opposed to informal caregiving arrangements made by families themselves [Harden et al. 1997]). Research suggests that almost one-third of all foster care placements are with relatives [Child Welfare League of America 1992] and that in larger states such as California and Illinois, from two-fifths to one-half of all foster care placements are with kin [Goerge et al. 1995]. Children of color, particularly African American children, are more likely to be placed with kin than are Caucasian children [Barth et al. 1994; Hegar & Scannapieco 1995], so that in many communities, a large percentage of African American children in foster care are being raised by extended family [Berrick et al. 1994; Dubowitz et al. 1993; Ingram 1996]. In the U.S. Department of Health and

Human Services' study [Harden et al. 1997], African American children were found to be eight times as likely as all other children to be living in formal kinship care arrangements.

A number of reasons have been given for the growing use of kinship care as a resource for children who are removed from the custody of their parents because of abuse or neglect. For African American children, there is a long history of extended family members caring for their kin's children [Stack 1974], with particular strengths among African American families in the adaptability of family roles and strong kinship bonds that support "taking in" of both blood and nonblood relatives temporarily or permanently [Hill 1972]. The literature describing patterns of caregiving in the African American community highlights traditions of self-help and community responsiveness to the needs of children [Billingsley 1992; Billingsley & Giovanni 1972; Everett et al. 1991; Hill 1977; Ross 1978].

Other reasons advanced for the growth in kinship care include the growing recognition among child welfare professionals that placement with relatives who feel a special commitment to a child's well-being can minimize the trauma to the child of being placed away from his or her parents [Dubowitz et al. 1993]. The preservation of family ties and continuity of both relationships and culture provided through kinship care have come to be seen as a significant strength for children [Berrick et al. 1994; Hegar & Scannapieco 1995; Ingram 1996]. Research also suggests that children in kinship care fare well, if not better, than children in other forms of out-of-home care. Data on kinship care suggest that placements with relatives tend to be quite stable [Courtney & Needell 1997; Goerge 1990], and although stays in care tend to be longer when compared to other forms of foster care [Barth et al. 1994; Goerge 1990], there is greater contact between the child and her parents [Berrick et al. 1994].

Although many children in kinship care achieve permanency through reunification with parents or long-term placement with relatives [Courtney & Needell 1997], formal adoption has been found to occur less frequently than among children in nonrelative care [Berrick et al. 1994; Dubowitz et al. 1993; Edmund Muskie

Institute 1995; Gleeson & Craig 1994]. Hill [2000] indicates that formal adoption by kin is more likely to occur when the child's birth parents have died, abandoned the child, or otherwise have little or no contact with the child or kin caregiver. Formal adoption often is not pursued when it would require the termination of the parental rights of a member of family who is involved with the child and caregiver at some level [Williams 1991].

Informal adoption, however, has been a common aspect of the close kinship bonds of African American families [Jackson-White et al. 1997]. Historically, as "a process whereby adult relatives or friends of the family took in children and cared for them when their parents were unable to provide for their needs" [Boyd-Franklin 1989, p. 52], informal adoption in the African American community traditionally has ensured that custody and responsibility for children has been transferred to other adults without severing parents' rights [Williams 1991]. Informal adoption in the African American community has taken the form of shared parenting to which, either explicitly or implicitly, the child's parent has agreed [Williams 1991]. In his study, Hill [1977] found in the mid-1970s that relatives—primarily grandparents, aunts, and uncles—had informally adopted over one million African American children.

The growing use of kinship care and its stability as demonstrated by the research suggests that rather than "languishing" in foster care, many African American children are in highly stable, committed living relationships with kin. As a consequence, it may be that many children whose statistical profiles reflect extended stays in care are already living with family and are not, as might be assumed on the basis of data related to length of care, in the "limbo" of foster care. For these children, formal adoption may or may not be appropriate or necessary, an issue currently being assessed in the context of efforts to implement and evaluate the use of subsidized guardianships as an alternative permanency option when children are with kin caregivers [Testa et al. 1996].

Although generally outside the scope of kinship care as it is typically defined, the role of relatives in relation to permanency for children in foster care arises in a second context—that is, when

children are placed with unrelated foster parents and become emotionally attached to them over time; adoption subsequently becomes
the permanency plan; and relatives then step forward expressing an
interest in adopting. The question in these circumstances is often
whether a relative should have "preferred" status as an adopter over
a nonrelated adult, including a foster parent with whom the child has
bonded and who wishes to adopt the child. This issue arises in its
most controversial form when a child has been cared for by unrelated
foster parents not of the child's race or culture who wish to adopt the
child, and a relative is then identified as an adoptive resource for the
child. Several cases presenting this issue recently have been featured
in the media. In a Minnesota case, the Caucasian foster parents of
an African American child, who had cared for her since she was four
days old, sought to adopt her and lost that opportunity when a court
ruled that the child's African American grandparents should have
custody [Coleman 1996]. In a Florida case, Caucasian foster parents,
who had cared for biracial fraternal twins for several years, sought to
adopt the twins and a paternal aunt of African American heritage
objected, seeking to adopt the twins herself [Associated Press 1997].
In a third case, the efforts of a Caucasian couple who are attempting
to adopt their foster son, who is both African American and Latino,
is being challenged by the child's African American cousin who
wishes to adopt him [Teicher 1999].

Legally, there has been no clear answer as to the respective
weight to be given, on the one hand, to relative status and the
family, racial, and cultural continuity that a relative would provide as an adoptive parent, and the weight to be given, on the other
hand, to a child's existing relationship with foster parents of a
different race and culture. Some states do not statutorily address
this issue, while in other states, statutes provide a preference for
relative adopters, requiring courts to first consider whether adoption by a relative is in a child's best interest [California Family
Code 1994; Colorado Children's Code 1993; Kansas Statutes Annotated 1993; Minnesota Statutes Annotated 1995]. Even in jurisdictions with statutory preferences for relatives, however, courts
retain considerable discretion in determining whether relatives
will be permitted to adopt [Oppenheim & Bussiere 1996].

The outcomes of cases from different jurisdictions demonstrate that courts vary in the weight they accord family bonds in adoption decision-making—and implicitly, the weight given to racial and cultural continuity in cases in which the current caregivers/prospective adoptive parents are not of the child's race or culture. Some courts have placed greater emphasis on the relationship with relatives than on the existing parent-child relationship with the child's foster parents [see *In the Matter of the Welfare of D.L.* 1992], while others have put greater weight on the foster parent's ability to meet a child's special needs as demonstrated over a substantial period of time [see *In re Stephanie M. 1994*]. Significant questions clearly remain on the extent to which relatives should have preferred status as adopters, either as a general principle or in individual situations. The divergent views reflected in courts' decisions provide the options with which practitioners and policymakers struggle: the position that kinship status alone is irrelevant; the view that the status of kin is one of several factors to consider; and the position that kinship bonds are a crucial factor in the "best interests of the child" determination.

Kinship care in general and preferences for kin at any level as prospective adoptive parents have drawn criticism from some advocates of transracial adoption. Some view kinship care as no more than a subterfuge to benefit the adults in a family [Kramer 1994; Sheindlin 1994] and both kinship care and relative preferences as a way to "subvert" the requirements of MEPA and limit the opportunities for transracial adoptions [National Council for Adoption 1997]. Bartholet [1998], for example, informed Congress in a hearing on interethnic adoption that:

> Kinship care has been promoted over the last couple of decades both because it keeps children within the extended family group and because, by doing so, it almost always keeps them within the racial groups as well. Policies favoring foster placement in the same community as the child's family of origin have been promoted on the grounds that they minimize disruption for the child, especially in cases where the child will eventually be

reunited with the birth family. But these policies also
generally serve to keep the child in its racial community
of origin, given neighborhood segregation patterns. . . .
Obviously, those who support kinship care and local
placement policies have a variety of motivations. But
there is no question but that for opponents of transracial
placement, these policies function as convenient end
runs around the new MEPA mandate.

This view of kin involvement with their children raises
significant issues. First, it suggests a value system that places great
weight on the perceived benefits of transracial adoption while
relegating kinship ties to a lower or even suspect level. It also
raises once again the question of whether policies promoting
transracial adoption are, at their core, grounded on concerns
related to meeting adult interests in adopting rather than children's
interests in a permanent family, particularly in view of the research indicating that children tend to fare well in what appear to
be, for the most part, highly stable kinship care arrangements
[Courtney & Needell 1997; Berrick et al. 1994; Goerge 1990]. An
objection to kinship care as an "end run" around transracial
adoption, in particular, may suggest an overarching concern with
promoting adult access to children whom they wish to adopt.
Perry [1990/1991, p. 119], for example, points to the great weight
given to the interests of adults with no existing relationship to a
child as compared to the weight given to the interests of the child
"where his racial needs and his needs for continuity, stability and
a permanent home are all being furthered," as is the case with
children's placements with kin.

Finally, objections to kinship care on the grounds that it may
defeat transracial adoption appear to misapprehend the continuing priority that federal law—the Adoption Assistance and Child
Welfare Act of 1980 and the Adoption and Safe Families Act of
1997—gives to family reunification as the primary permanency
goal for children in foster care [42 U.S.C. § 671(a)(15)(B)]. From
both a policy and practice perspective, kinship care and placement of children in their own communities have been viewed as

building on important extended family and community relationships to maximize opportunities for timely reunification of children with their parents, or if not with their parents, with members
of their extended families [Hornby et al. 1996]. In the legal
framework of permanency alternatives, adoption and other permanency alternatives are to be considered only after these alternatives are determined to be inappropriate or unavailable [42 U.S.C.
§ 671(a)(15)(C].

The more likely dangers associated with "end runs" would
appear to be activities associated with legal efforts to pressure
child welfare agencies and the courts to authorize transracial
adoptions in cases in which reunification remains a viable alternative. In the 1999 case of *Baby T.*, for example, a court ruling in
favor of reunification of a child with his African American mother
over the objections of his Caucasian foster parents who wished to
adopt him triggered a federal investigation in which violations of
MEPA were alleged [Lehmann 1999]. The charge that race was
improperly taken into account in the decision to reunify the child
with a parent whom the court determined to be "fit" suggests
potential dangers associated with the use of race-based criteria to
circumvent reunification of children with their own parents. If
race-based factors can be utilized in this context, it would appear
that they could likewise be used in cases of kinship care to defeat
children's placements with relatives in favor of Caucasian families who wish to adopt them.

It is clear that kinship care does not and cannot provide
permanency for all children of color in foster care [Ingram 1996].
Its increasing use, however, and the positive outcomes for children associated with kinship care suggest that there are important
lessons to be learned regarding the extent to which the interests of
children of color in foster care can be met by continuing connections with their family and cultural community. The benefits of
family and cultural continuity provided to children of color
through kinship care represent important dynamics in any consideration of the role of race and culture in permanency planning for
children in foster care.

Adoption of Children of Color by Same-Race Families

For children of color in foster care who cannot or will not be reunited with their parents and for whom kinship care does not offer permanency, an essential alternative is adoption by families of children's own race and culture. Virtually all researchers, including those who have found that children are not harmed psychologically by transracial adoption placements, have concluded that, whenever possible, children should be placed for adoption with families of their own race and culture [see Gill & Jackson 1983; Grow & Shapiro 1974; Simon & Altstein 1987]. Rather than questioning the benefits of same race placements, the concern that is frequently expressed is that adoptive families of color are not available in sufficient numbers to meet the needs of all waiting children of color [Barth 1997]. The practice literature, however, suggests that factors other than demographic sufficiency are more powerful in undermining the extent to which families of color have served or will serve in the future as adoptive resources for children of color in foster care.

The literature is almost uniform in highlighting the benefits of placing a child adoptively with a family of his or her own race and culture [Committee for Hispanic Children and Families 1996; Johnson et al. 1987; McRoy & Zurcher 1983; Simon & Altstein 1987] because of the family's ability to meet the child's "diverse interests in continuity, stability, and racial identity" [Perry 1990/1991, p. 110]. Despite the overall positive outcomes associated with transracial adoption, the more negative findings related to adoptees' racial identity formation, adjustment difficulties, and negative perceptions of other African Americans suggest that adoptive placements that offer ethnic similarity between parents and child optimize outcomes for children. Perry [1990/1991, p. 118], for example, writes:

> The child's various interests converge when he is placed for adoption with parents of the same race. His interest in a healthy and positive racial identity is most effectively furthered. At the same time, this approach does not detrimentally affect his other interests. The child has an interest in being placed in a permanent home. This

interest is not undermined by the consideration of race where race operates as a preference rather than a bar.

Because of the convergence of children's interests when they are placed with families of their own race and culture, the majority of researchers and scholars have viewed in-race adoptions as preferable for children and transracial adoptions as resources for children only when families of the child's own race and culture cannot be found [Johnson et al. 1987; McRoy & Zurcher 1983; Simon & Altstein 1987].

This view of the overall benefits of same race placement, however, is not uniformly held. Bartholet [1991], for example, asserts that Caucasian families are not only equally capable of raising African American children to be healthy, well-adjusted adults but may have a greater ability to do so. She writes, based on what appear to be beliefs that African American families operate essentially from a "deficit" perspective, that Caucasian adopters of African American children are uniquely privileged, and that the primary benefit bestowed on adopted children by their adoptive parents is material advantage:

> There is no evidence that Black parents do a better job than white parents of raising black children with a sense of pride in their racial heritage and culture. . . Critics of transracial adoption have claimed that only blacks can teach black children the coping skills needed for life in a racist society, but there seems at least as good an argument for the proposition that whites are in the best position to teach black children how to maneuver in the white worlds of power and privilege. Indeed it seems clear that for black children growing up in a white-dominated world, there would be a range of material advantages associated with having white parents and living in the largely white and relatively privileged world that such parents tend to frequent [1991, p. 1221].

This position is not broadly expressed in mainstream literature but may reflect some of the underlying sentiments of those who ardently advocate for broader use of transracial adoption.

More commonly, issues related to placement of African American children with African American adoptive families focus on the extent to which the African American community can provide adoptive resources for these children. Formal adoption is a relatively recent phenomenon for African Americans, a fact based in a historical context in which for many decades, "the dominant child welfare institutions of the country openly excluded Black children" [Billingsley & Giovanni 1972, p. 213] and African Americans were not encouraged to consider adoption [Williams 1991]. Within the African American community in the early part of the 20th century, however, there was a pattern of third-party, interstate adoption practice in which African American lawyers assisted single, pregnant middle-class African American women to place their children for adoption [Williams 1991]. Although it is not clear whether this practice involved informal arrangements or legalized adoptions [Williams 1991], it does suggest that the African American community in the early part of this century developed its own services to respond to the needs of pregnant African American women for whom extended family assistance was not a desirable option.

It was not until the late 1960s and early 1970s that adoption began to be made available as a formal service for African American children [Williams 1991]. In the 1950s and early 1960s, foster care was the primary service for African American children. Adoption was provided principally as a service for Caucasian children [Jeter 1963], largely because adoption historically had been a service provided by voluntary adoption agencies to childless white couples, not a service provided to poor children in need of families [McRoy 1989]. As noted by Morgenstern [1971, p. 68], until the late 1960s, "official agency adoptions had been considered almost exclusively a white middle class affair," although there were some exceptions such as the placement of African American infants by Spence Chapin Adoption Services in New York City in the late 1940s [Spence Chapin 1947].

Although some writers point to the civil rights advances of the 1960s and 1970s as promoting greater access to adoption services for African American children [Williams 1991], others emphasize the substantial increase in the number of African American families reported to the public child welfare system during that era as mandatory reporting laws were enacted [Howard 1984]; poverty-related neglect became a basis for state intervention [Howe 1997]; and child welfare services became "dominated by the process of legislating, implementing and publicizing child abuse reporting laws and expanding the definition of abuse" [Kamerman 1998/1999, p. 5]. Children of color were particularly affected by these developments, as poor families were more likely to fall under the surveillance of child welfare authorities [Howard 1984]. As the number of children of color in foster care grew, their stays lengthened, and the psychological impact of impermanency on children became apparent, emphasis began to be placed on delivering adoption services for African American children [Billingsley & Giovanni 1972; Day 1979]. These children, however, were viewed as "hard to place" [Billingsley & Giovanni 1972] and have continued to be considered as harder to place for adoption than other children [Chipungu 1991]. Virtually every state, for example, includes membership in a minority group within its definition of "special needs" (which must, under federal law, identify those characteristics of children that make it reasonable to conclude that they cannot be placed for adoption without financial assistance for their adoptive families) [Avery 1998].

In response to the growing number of African American children in the child welfare system in the 1960s and 1970s, agencies became more interested in recruiting African American adoptive families. Through mid-century, agencies approved few African American prospective adoptive parents and made few adoptive placements with them. A Child Welfare League of America study of adoptions through a major Pittsburgh agency conducted in the 1950s, for example, found that fewer than one-fifth of African American adoptive applicants completed adoptions compared to two-fifths of the Caucasian applicants [Gill, in press]. The successful African American applicants attended an average of 12.7 interviews before being allowed to adopt [Gill, in press]. Even as agencies began to make greater efforts to recruit African American families in the late 1960s, they reported difficulties in finding appropriate African American adoptive applicants. A study of agencies in a major urban area conducted in the 1960s found that agencies rejected one-fourth of the African American adoptive family applicants even though they had a backlog of waiting African American children needing families [Gill, in press].

Just as African American children came to be labeled "hard to place," African American families came to be characterized as "hard to reach" [Billingsley & Giovanni 1972]. Many who have critically examined agencies' reported problems in recruiting African American families have rejected the explanation that African American families are difficult to engage and have attributed the problems instead to systemic and programmatic issues within the agencies themselves [Jackson-White et al. 1997; McRoy et al. 1997; Brown & Bailey-Etta 1997]. Specifically, these writers have associated the difficulties of traditional adoption agencies in effectively reaching this population of families with the agencies' lack of experience in providing services to African American families, their mistaken pathologizing of the strengths of African American families, and agency policies that automatically screened out unmarried persons and individuals over 40 years of age from consideration as adoptive parents [Jackson-White et al. 1997]. Some writers have questioned the appropriateness of traditional adoption agencies attempting to serve African American children in the first place. Duncan [1993], for example, writes:

> I believe that if we were to seek answers for Anglo-American children who needed adoptive families, we would not envision the solution as being within the African American agencies and expect this to be the most sensible means to solve their problem. Yet, this is precisely what is happening in terms of black children. Traditionally white agencies, with histories of refusing service to black children as recently as 12 or 15 years ago, are now the primary caretakers and planners for children who are black. It should be noted that an enormous amount of money is involved in supporting these agen-

cies. Funding sources for adoption services are investing resources in training white staff to serve black children rather than investing in the African-American Community and its agencies. When the African American Community is appropriately permitted to be involved in the adoption needs of black children, the most significant barrier to their being adopted will be removed and the problem solved.

The enactment of the Adoption Assistance and Child Welfare Act (P.L. 96-272) in 1980 and the development of effective programs on the part of adoption agencies in the private sector led to gains in the early to mid-1980s in the recruitment of African American families for African American children [Jackson-White et al. 1997]. Specialized African American adoption agencies, beginning with the founding of Homes for Black Children in Detroit, and community-based advocacy programs began to demonstrate that recruitment efforts targeted at African American families could be successful [Williams 1991]. A 1990-1991 national survey of 87 agencies in 25 states, for example, found that private agencies specializing in recruiting African American families succeeded in placing 94% of their African American children with these families [Gilles & Kroll 1991]. Success on the part of agencies that specialized in recruiting families of color was associated with personalized presentations of children, culturally sensitive adoption staff, the availability of adoption subsidies, support for single individuals interested in adopting, use of foster care-adoptive placements, and active work with communities about the needs of children for adoptive families [Gilles & Kroll 1991]. Despite the success of these programs, however, the growth in the number of children of color in foster care continued at such a level that individual community-based recruitment efforts were not able to keep pace with the need [Williams 1991].

Barriers to effective recruitment of African American and Latino families have been the focus of both research and the adoption literature. The 1990-1991 national survey of adoption agencies found that 83% of the agencies were aware of barriers that discouraged or prevented families of color from adopting [Gilles & Kroll 1991]. The barriers most frequently cited were few people of color in agencies' staff and managerial positions, inadequate recruitment efforts in communities of color, rigid adherence to standards that were believed to represent the "ideal" in adoptive families, fees for adoption, and negative views of adoption agencies by families of color [Gilles & Kroll 1991]. Similarly, a study by Rodriquez and Meyer [1990] found that agency policies, staffing patterns, and community perceptions of the agencies served as obstacles to recruitment of families of color for older children of color in care. A recent survey of Mexican Americans [Bausch & Serpe, 1999] found that structural barriers to adoption—the lack of information about adoption, limited financial support for adoptive families, and the failure of agencies to have bilingual staff in place—were far greater impediments to adoption by Mexican Americans than the cultural barriers associated with familism and machismo.

The use of fees has been identified as a particularly troubling issue for African American adopters, violating the cultural values of families of color because of the association of adoption fees with the historical practice of buying and selling African American children [Rodriquez & Meyer 1990]. The charging of fees also raises issues related to the respective "value" of African American children as compared to Caucasian children. This issue takes its most disconcerting form in private agency fee schedule practices that advertise fees for African American children at a lower level than fees for Caucasian children [Foster 1997]. Poussaint [cited in Foster 1997, p. A1] has commented that such practices imply that African American children are being sold "cheap," with the "better-quality babies" costing more.

The issue of the extent to which African Americans have been approved as adoptive families has been the subject of some debate. A number of studies suggest low approval rates of African Americans applicants [Gill, in press; Rodriquez & Meyer 1990]. Some advocates of transracial adoption, however, maintain that the reverse is the case. In her testimony to Congress, for example,

Bartholet [1998] asserted that agencies, prior to the enactment of MEPA, had routinely approved African American families but not Caucasian families solely on the basis of those families' race:

> Race matching had been one of the most important decision-making criteria ... Race had outweighed virtually all other parental fitness factors, and social workers had drastically altered their traditional selection criteria for minority race adopters, in their desperation to find same-race matches for the waiting black children.

A review of existing data and research has not yielded any empirical support for these assertions. No data has been found that substantiates the claim that Caucasian families applying to adopt have been rejected, as a group, from consideration as prospective adoptive parents for African American children in foster care on the basis of race. Nor has evidence been found that supports the claim that African Americans have been approved as adopters under significantly modified assessment criteria that create risks of harm for children.

In contrast to Bartholet's assertion that there has been widespread recruitment of African American families using minimal assessment criteria [1998], other transracial adoption proponents such as Murphy [1998] assert that the number of recruited families from the African American community has not been nor ever will be sufficient to meet the current and future need. Murphy [1998] in his testimony to Congress on interethnic adoptions, stated:

> [Y]ou need only look at the numbers. ... Again, the deck is stacked against African American children. In Cook County, approximately 88% of the 40,000 foster children are African American, while only about one-third of the County's residents are black ... [F]or every white child who is in foster care, there are about 900 other white people of all ages who are not in state custody. For every Hispanic kid in the child welfare system, there are 400 Hispanic people who are not in foster care. But for every black foster child, there are only about 45 black men,

women, and children who are not in foster care. To make matters worse, this small number is reduced by the disproportionate number of black men who are in state custody, as prisoners.

This type of population-based analysis does not appear to take into account critical factors contributing to permanency for African American children: kinship relationships and commitment of extended family to the care of children; family resources outside the immediate community; and the availability of adoptive families unrelated to the child in other counties and states (for whom, under the Adoption and Safe Families Act, geographical barriers to adoption are to be removed).

Arguments based on a purported demographic insufficiency within communities of color may rely less on empirical data and more on conventional notions that African Americans have little interest in formal adoption [see Howe 1997]. Despite popular assumptions, a number of studies suggest that members of the African American community have a high level of interest in formal adoption. The Black Pulse Surveys conducted by Hill [1981, 1993] have indicated that three million African American households are interested in adoption. A more recent survey by the National Urban League found that one-third of African American household heads indicated an interest in the formal adoption of an African American child [Hill 1997]. Other surveys have found that African Americans are as likely as Caucasians to adopt children [U.S. National Center for Health Statistics 1990] or more likely [Mason & Williams 1985]. Gershenson [1984], for example, compared the rate of adoption by African American families above the poverty level to the rate of adoption by Caucasian families and found a higher rate among African American families (18 per 10,000) than among Caucasian families (4 per 10,000). Similarly, other studies suggest that when social class is controlled, African Americans formally adopt at higher rates than comparable Caucasian families [Family Impact Seminar 1998; Mason & Williams 1985].

A final issue that warrants attention in the context of adoptive resources for children of color in foster care is the question of "same race" adoptive placements for Caucasian children and the extent to which considerations of race and culture apply to these children and their prospective adoptive parents. As Brooks and colleagues [1997, p. 5] point out, race has been "routinely considered in the placement of Caucasian children (i.e., Caucasian children are rarely placed transracially)." In the context of the transracial adoption debate, is this reality subject to examination and remediation? Do MEPA requirements prohibiting considerations related to race, color, and national origin in adoptive placements also mean that Caucasian children—who currently comprise 32% of the waiting children in foster care—should have an equal opportunity to be adopted by an African American or Latino family? If not, is the question, then, as Kroll [1998] rhetorically asks, "Would anyone suggest that white children are being discriminated against because they do not have the same opportunity to be adopted out of race as children of color?"

Perry [1994/1994, p. 103] notes that this issue has been "essentially avoided" by those who promote transracial adoption practice. Observing that the issue may be deemed "irrelevant" because of the larger number of African American children waiting in foster care and the fact that African Americans generally tend to adopt African American children, she nonetheless emphasizes the "symbolic importance" of this issue to the African American community [1993/1994, p. 103]. She contends that there is importance in asking not only what adults may choose to do but what they "have the right to do" [1993/1994, p. 104]. Arguing that there is a profound discrepancy as to how adoptive resources are viewed for the two populations of Caucasian children and African American children, she writes:

> It seems clear that advocates of transracial adoption are not in fact arguing for a system based on colorblindness . . . Instead, they affirm a system based on racial choice. Under this system, race apparently still can be used to match white families with their choice of the valuable commodity of a white baby. White families are, of course, free to select Black children for adoption. The problem, however, is that this principle operates only one way.

Choosing across racial lines is reserved for whites. Under the choice system, are Black families similarly free to adopt white children? It appears that advocates of color-blind individualism believe that the idea merits little discussion. Thus, they really advocate a system in which white children are reserved for white families, white families have the opportunity to choose to adopt Black children or white children, and Black potential adoptive parents may choose Black children [1993/1994, p. 104].

This issue, by requiring an examination of the needs of waiting children of all races and societal beliefs about who should adopt whom, raises fundamental questions about the role of race and culture in adoption. If, as MEPA unequivocally states, race does not matter, should not Caucasian children be placed as readily with families of color as minority children are placed with Caucasian families? From the perspective of the adults involved, should all adults have equal opportunity to adopt any individual child? Or is there a "system of choice" that differentially vests power based on the race of adopters despite the ostensible commitment to "colorblindness?" And if there is a differential system for adopters, is there also a hierarchal system for children, in which Caucasian children are valued more highly than African American children and, therefore, entitled to ostensibly "better," that is, Caucasian adoptive families?

The Needs of Children Already Placed With Foster Parents of a Different Race and Culture

A separate issue from that of the role of race and culture in selecting adoptive families for children of color with whom the children have no prior relationship is the question of the best interests of a child of color already placed transracially with a foster family who, when the child becomes free for adoption, wishes to adopt her. Unlike an infant to be placed with an adoptive family with whom there is no existing relationship, a child of color with an established relationship with his or her foster parents has, in addition to race-based needs related to identity and self-esteem, nonrace needs related to the continuity of an existing nurturing parent-child relationship. In some cases, these children also will have special health and developmental needs that have been well met by their foster parents over a significant period of time. These needs in transracial foster care/prospective adoptive placements present potentially competing interests requiring a weighing of relative importance.

It would appear that situations involving children who live with foster families who wish to adopt them are "conceptually and analytically separate" from situations involving the initial adoptive placements of children [Perry 1993/1994, p. 95]. Because foster care situations raise important concerns about the disruption of long-established, caring parent-child relationships, these cases extend beyond consideration of race and color—which may be a key issue in decision making about adoptive placements in which no prior parent-child relationship exists and the child's race-based needs do not require a balancing against other interests. As Perry [1993/1994, p. 94] states, cases involving the adoption of children in foster care "raise the question of the weight race should be given when Black children have been placed with white families for sufficiently long periods of time to form psychological bonds with them."

Nonetheless, the distinctions between situations involving adoptions by foster parents and situations involving initial adoptive placements of infants have not been made clear in the debates surrounding transracial adoption. At the same time, policies related to the role of race and culture in adoption largely have been reactive, responding to decisions made by child welfare agencies or courts that deny individual Caucasian foster families the opportunity to adopt children of color after caring for them for years [see *Drummond v. Fulton* 1978]. Anecdotal accounts of situations in which foster parent-child relationships were disrupted in order to place children with adoptive families of children's same race and culture have been used to make the case that race and culture should play no role whatsoever in making adoptive placements for children [Brooks et al. 1999; Metzenbaum 1995].

Many, however, who maintain that race and culture should matter in making an initial adoptive placement, give race and culture less weight in cases involving adoption by a child's foster parents. General agreement appears to exist regarding the negative psychological impact on children when parent-child bonds are disrupted [Watkins 1987; Center for Early Education and Development 1991], an impact seen as so substantial as to lead many writers to advocate placing lesser weight on the race and culture based needs of children in such situations. Kroll [1998], for example, in his testimony before Congress recommended as a "common sense guiding principle" that "children should not be moved from a stable and loving placement for any reason, including racial matching." Duncan [1993] highlights the individual needs of children, writing that despite her commitment to policymaking and planning for African American children in need of adoption being based in the African American community, "the decision about a home for a specific child must be based on his particular needs and circumstances." Perry [1990/1991, p. 104] balances continuity and raced-based needs as follows:

> It is preferable to leave the child with long-term caretakers when his racial needs conflict with his needs for continuity of care. First, although social scientists seem to agree that all things being equal, a Black child is better off in a Black home, where a child has already lived for a substantial period of time with one of the families, all things are not equal. The fact that one set of adults already has a relationship with the child is a factor that is significant given the needs of the child for stability.

These issues, which raise the need to weigh and prioritize one set of children's needs against another set of interests, emphasize the importance of the choices that are made regarding initial foster care placements for children of color. If, as virtually all the research and literature suggests, a same-race placement is in the child's best interests when all things are otherwise equal, then foster care placements for children when they first enter care should take into account children's race- and culture-based needs, particularly when there is reason to believe that reunification with parents or placement with relatives will not be reasonable alternatives [McRoy 1994]. The critical factors associated with children's positive sense of racial identity in foster care situations—the racial environment and the attitudes of the foster family and peers, the race of other children in care with the child, the age of the child, race socialization experiences, and the child's stage of racial identity development [Rotheram & Phinney 1987; Semaj 1985; Peters 1985; Phinney et al. 1990]—individually and collectively highlight the important benefits to children provided by same-race foster parents [McRoy 1996]. Particularly with the growing use of concurrent planning and foster/adoptive placements to expedite adoption when reunification will not be further pursued [Katz 1999], the initial foster care placement—and attention to the racial and cultural identity needs of children at time of foster care placement—has become increasingly important in the permanency planning process. The prohibitions of MEPA related to the consideration of race, color, and national origin in foster care placements as well as adoption, however, raise serious concerns about the extent to which current policy may work against thoughtful and critical longer-term planning for children.

In those situations in which a child's needs for continuity and stability in a long-standing parent-child relationship are deemed paramount and the child is transracially adopted, there is broad agreement that children's race- and culture-based needs must be recognized and addressed [Crumbley 1998; Mascareñas 1997; McRoy 1994; Bower 1998]. In the Report by the Adoption and Race Work Group convened by the Stuart Foundation, Brooks and colleagues [1997, p. 25] set forth as guiding principles that assessments of children who are transracially adopted should be "responsive to [children's] cultural backgrounds" and that assessments of prospective adoptive parents should "consist of the families' ability to nurture, support and reinforce a given child's physical and psychological well-being, including the child's racial, ethnic, and cultural identity. The families' capacity to help a given child cope with all forms of discrimination, including that due to the child's racial, ethnic, and cultural background, should also be assessed." Similarly, clinical experts have highlighted the range of issues that impact children and families in transracial adoptions, including Crumbley [1998] who notes that attention must be paid to the child and the adoptive family's needs to develop racial identities for both the child and the family; the parenting skills, knowledge, resources, and capability needed to provide an adoptee with racial and cultural identity; and the child's need for a positive racial identity in order to function well in a race-conscious and discriminatory society.

Although the Office of Civil Rights has interpreted MEPA as precluding special training and/or preparation of families who adopt transracially [Pollack 1998], the clinical and professional social work literature suggests that transracial adoption presents unique parental tasks [Bower 1998] and that families who adopt transracially will need assistance in helping their children to develop "positive racial self-feelings" [McRoy 1994, p. 71]. Consistently, experts from the African American community have emphasized that in order to promote African American children's psychological development and well-being, their parents must be able to engage in a direct discussion of race and racism with their children [Chestang 1983; Comer & Poussaint 1975; Hopson & Hopson 1990; Pinderhughes 1989]. Similarly, Mascareñas [1997, p. 67] focuses on the needs of Latino children who are adopted transculturally to develop "healthy and intact coping skills to deal with a racist world." Crumbley [1998] outlines the critical importance of parents' acknowledging the existence of prejudice, racism, and discrimination; explaining to their child why his or her minority group is mistreated; preparing the child for discrimination, including providing the child with a repertoire of responses to racial discrimination; giving the child role models and positive contact with the child's minority community; teaching the child the difference between responsibility to and for his or her minority group; and advocating on behalf of the child's positive identity. The National Association of Black Social Workers [1996], likewise, acknowledging that there are some children who must be placed transracially, emphasizes that:

[I]t must be remembered that white adoptive families become "mixed" families after they adopt transracially. They have to be given pre- and post-adoption services to enable them to help their children cope with racism and culture of origin disconnection. Many transracial adoptees bemoan the fact that their adoptive parents were ill-equipped to help them with these issues and that their self-esteem suffered as a result.

Clearly, there will be instances in which children of color will be served by transracial adoption—children who have been reared by foster families not of their race or culture who wish to adopt them and children of color freed for adoption for whom, despite concerted efforts, no adoptive family of their own race and culture has been found. Although in such circumstances, children's race- and culture- based needs may be determined to have lesser weight than their needs for continuity and/or permanency, their race- and culture-based needs are significant, raising ethical questions related to their "best interests" when efforts are made to ignore or minimize these core identity issues.

Summary

As this analysis of the role of race and culture in the adoption of children of color in foster care suggests, transracial adoption may, at best, offer a limited resource for some children and, at worst, deflect attention from the complex, pressing problems that bring children of color disproportionately into foster care and keep them in care for extended periods of time. Studies have consistently shown that entry into foster care is closely associated with poverty [Pelton 1994; Hollingsworth 1998], inadequate housing [National Black Child Development Institute 1989] and parental substance abuse [Vega et al. 1993], issues which transracial adoption policy in no way addresses. Perry notes that despite the "symbolic significance of transracial adoption" and the controversy surrounding the issue, in the end, it does not provide "a solution to the many problems that the vast majority of Black

children in this society face" [1993/1994, p. 107]. Similarly, the
president of the local Chicago chapter of the National Association
of Black Social Workers concludes that "keeping black children
out of foster care" is more important than focusing on transracial
adoption [Forte 1997, p. 21].

However, as Courtney [1997] notes, advocates of transracial
adoption as the "solution" to achieving permanency for children
of color in foster care largely have ignored the social realities
associated with children's entry into foster care, given these issues
a bare mention, or concluded that nothing can or will be done
about these problems anyway. Also noting the dearth of attention
given by transracial adoption proponents to the broader system's
issues and the racial and cultural environment in which they
occur, Perry questions whether, in the end, transracial adoption is
"really about the interests of Black children at all" [1993/1994, p.
107].

Whether the goal for the future is framed as giving special
attention to the needs of families and children of color "given the
child welfare system's long history of ignoring or misconstruing
their needs" [Courtney 1997, p. 768] or as moving "the debate back
to the interests of children and go[ing] beyond theoretical or
political debate" [Perry 1993/1994, p. 107], there are key questions
to be considered and a broader knowledge base to be developed.
The following questions, adapted from McRoy [1989, p. 157-158],
bear on the role of race and culture in the adoption of children in
foster care and present some of the key challenges for the future:

- Is there a genuine commitment to reducing the number
  of African American and other children of color who
  enter the foster care system?

- Are agencies' services as accessible to families of color
  as they are to Caucasian families?

- To what extent do the interests of prospective adoptive
  parents with regard to the type of children whom they
  wish to adopt shape policies related to the role that race
  and culture should play in adoption?

- Is racial matching an acceptable criterion for some children but not others?

- How do agencies determine the suitability of a family to foster and adopt a child not of their same race and culture? Is the ability to support and promote a positive racial identity for the transracially adopted child an important criterion?

- To what extent should the law, in its current form as MEPA, govern how decisions are made with regard to the adoptive placements of children of color?

These questions can best be answered through the development of a broader knowledge base: improved data and sources of data, including methodologically sound research; collection of qualitative information from the children, families, and communities served through adoption [see Ortega et al. 1996]; the identification of "best-in-class" programs that effectively achieve permanency for children and promote their racial and cultural identity needs; and rigorous examination of the systemic forces that impede permanence for children of color.

Part II

The Role of Culture in the Adoption of American Indian Children

Although race and culture have played important roles in the adoption of African American, Latino, and other children of color, culture—by virtue of both history and legislative action—has played a unique role in the adoption of American Indian children in the United States. The extent to which cultural considerations have shaped and continue to define the nature of adoption for Indian children has, in large part, been directed by the Indian Child Welfare Act of 1978 (ICWA) (P.L. 95-608). ICWA and the reasons for its enactment contrast sharply with the Multi-Ethnic Placement Act of 1994 (P.L 103-382) and the subsequent Interethnic Placement Act Amendments of 1996 (P.L. 104-188) (collectively MEPA) and the concerns leading to the enactment of those laws. MEPA, which minimizes the role of race and, by extension, culture in children's foster care and adoption placements, was enacted in an attempt to increase the number of adoptive families for children of color (expressly excluding Indian children). The Indian Child Welfare Act, in direct contrast, acknowledges the vital importance of Indian children's cultural heritage in the provision of foster care and adoption services and was enacted to halt the systematic unwarranted separation of Indian children from their families and cultural communities.

The Historical Context: Child Welfare Practice and Enactment of ICWA

Since the late 1800s, policy regarding American Indians concentrated on suppression of American Indian culture and assimilation of American Indians into mainstream U.S. culture [Howard 1984]. Separation of Indian children from their families, communities, and tribes was the cornerstone of this policy, and one of the core strategies was the placement of Indian children in distant boarding schools for purposes of education and "civilization" [Guerrero 1979; Thompson 1990]. Boarding schools provided controlled environments in which children lived for years with no contact with their families or tribes, making it possible to divest children of all remnants of tribal identity [Howard 1984]. As Horejsi and colleagues [1992, pp. 333–334] observe, "clearly, the boarding school was an effort to destroy cultural identity; unfortunately, it was quite successful."

The suppression of Indian culture and assimilation of Indian children into non-Indian cultural environments through boarding school placements of children coincided with policies that supported the removal of Indian children from their families and tribes on grounds related to child protection. Historically, allegations of child neglect were utilized to remove Indian children from their families and tribes and place them with non-Indian families or in institutions, in most cases never to be returned to their families or culture [Howard 1984]. These practices did not come under serious scrutiny until the 1970s when the American Indian Policy Review Commission ("he Commission"), established by Congress at the urging of Indian tribes, closely examined a range of federal and state policies that impacted Indian tribes, including state agencies' interventions into Indian families [Thorne 1999]. The 1977 final report of the Commission concluded that " [r]emoval of Indian children from their cultural setting seriously impacts long-term tribal survival and has damaging social and psychological impact on many individual Indian children" [Senate Report 1977, p. 52]. In a Congressional hearing held in conjunction with the release of the Commission's report, William Byler [1977], executive director of the Association on American Indian Affairs, described "the wholesale separation of [Indian] children from their families," and in a statement that mirrored the concerns of American Indian leaders such as Issac [1978], concluded that "[i]t is clear then that the Indian child welfare crisis is of massive proportions and that Indian families face vastly greater risks of involuntary separation than are typical of our society as a whole."

By the 1970s, a quarter or more of American Indian children had been removed from their families and placed in foster care, in institutions, or with adoptive families—a placement rate from 5 to 19 times greater than for non-Indian children [Byler 1977]. As many as 85% of the Indian children removed from their families had been placed in non-Indian foster homes, and as many as 90% of Indian children had been adopted by non-Indian families [House of Representatives Report 1978].

In addition to concerns about the number of Indian children removed from their families and cultural environments, attention focused on the vague grounds on which these actions were based, generally "neglect," "social deprivation," and "emotional damage" that children purportedly suffered as a result of living with their parents [Gallagher 1994, p. 85; MacEachron et al. 1996, p. 453]. Whether because of unfamiliarity with or hostility to an unfamiliar Indian culture, social workers evaluated Indian families on the basis of standards that did not take into account culturally different child-rearing practices [MacEachron et al. 1996], and non-Indian judges failed to appreciate the cultural differences between American Indian communities and "the norms of white, middle class society" [Hollinger 1989, pp. 454–455]. Social workers and judges viewed American Indian parenting practices of leaving children with adults outside the nuclear family as neglect, and, in some cases, as a sufficient basis for terminating parental rights. McCarthy [1996, p. B8] has noted that:

> It was overlooked that in tribal cultures the amount of care given a child went well beyond one household. The full social and blood-tie network of parents, grandparents, relatives and neighbors was a wealth not categorized on a caseworker's clipboard of acceptable standards for child-raising.

Other Indian child-rearing practices, such as the greater permissiveness of Indian parents and the assignment of responsibilities to children earlier in their lives than would typically be the case in European American families, were likewise considered indicators of harmful neglect [Howard 1984].

Child welfare authorities and the courts also tended to view social conditions such as poverty and alcoholism more negatively for Indian families than non-Indian families [MacEachron et al. 1996]. Poverty, a significant by-product of the reservation system with economic, cultural, and social effects [Kunesh 1996], served in many instances as the sole basis for removal of Indian children. McCarthy [1996, p. B8], for example, has noted that "on many reservations, it was once enough for caseworkers to decide arbitrarily that a family was too poor to raise a child." Alcohol abuse, a major health problem among American Indians [Horejsi 1987], likewise played a significant role in child welfare decision-making. Although parental abuse of alcohol is a serious indicator of potential risk in Indian and non-Indian homes, studies suggested that alcohol abuse in an Indian home was more likely to lead to the removal of the child from the home than was the case if the home were non-Indian [House of Representatives Report 1978].

In response to "the widespread destruction of American Indian families that had reached epidemic proportions by the 1970s," [Bennett 1993, p. 955], the Indian Child Welfare Act was enacted in 1978:

> To protect the best interests of Indian children and to promote the stability and security of Indian tribes and families by the establishment of minimum Federal standards for the removal of Indian children from their families and the placement of such children in foster or adoptive homes which will reflect the unique values of Indian culture, and providing for assistance to Indian tribes in the operation of child and family services programs [25 U.S.C. § 1902].

ICWA was based on findings that the states had failed "to recognize the essential tribal relations of Indian people and the cultural and social standards prevailing in Indian communities and families" and that, as a consequence, "an alarmingly high percentage of Indian families are broken up by the removal, often unwarranted, of their children from them" and "an alarmingly high percentage of such children are placed in non-Indian foster and adoptive homes and institutions" [§ 1901]. The excessive number of involuntary removals by state agencies of Indian children from their families and their tribes and these agencies' placements of Indian children with non-Indian families were clearly the critical problems that ICWA was designed primarily to address.

The Act, however, also addressed situations in which Indian parents made voluntary decisions to place their children for adoption [§ 1911(a), § 1913, § 1915]. Congress recognized that economic, religious, and social incentives could prompt Indian parents to place their children for adoption, decisions that might be in opposition to or outweighed by the best interests of Indian children, families, and the cultural community [Watts 1989]. Testimony in Congressional hearings on ICWA indicated that abuses had occurred in voluntary placements of children by Indian parents: social workers in some cases threatened Indian parents that welfare payments would be withheld if they did not give their consent to adoption; missionaries encouraged Indians to allow their children to be adopted so that they would be "rescued" from the "heathen" reservations on which they were born; and financial benefits were offered to induce poor Indian parents to place their children for adoption in order to respond to a growing demand among Caucasians for infants to adopt [Senate Report 1977]. In response to these issues, ICWA broadly includes within its scope "any child custody proceeding" [§ 1911], including a "voluntary termination of parental rights" [§ 1913].

The Specific Provisions of ICWA

ICWA contains both substantive and procedural provisions related to foster care for and the adoption of Indian children. Each of these provisions has provoked debate, with many of the issues centering on the appropriateness of the Act's emphasis on the value of Indian culture in the context of foster care and adoptive placements for Indian children. Briefly, the key substantive provisions are as follows:

- ICWA applies to any "Indian child," a term defined in the Act as a child who is "(a) a member of an Indian tribe, or (b) eligible for membership in an Indian tribe and is the biological child of a member of an Indian tribe" [25 U.S.C. §1903].

- ICWA applies to all "child custody proceedings" involving Indian children: foster care, preadoption and adoptive placements, and termination of parental rights proceedings [§ 1903]. Only two exceptions are recognized: custody proceedings relating to divorce decrees if custody is awarded to one parent and cases in which a juvenile has committed an act which if committed by an adult would be a crime [§ 1903].

- The "preferencing section" of the ICWA, which Carleton calls the "real bite" of the Act [1997, p. 26], orders the priority by which Indian children are to be placed in foster care and with adoptive families [§1915]. When adoption is sought for a American Indian child, ICWA requires that the child be placed with a member of the child's extended family; if such a placement is not feasible, the child is to be placed with another member of the same Indian tribe as the child; and if neither opportunity exists, as a final alternative, the child is to be placed with another Indian family. In foster care placements, ICWA provides that an Indian child is first to be placed with a member of the child's extended family; if that is not possible, the child is to be placed in a foster home licensed, approved or specified by the child's tribe, or as the next alternative, in an Indian foster home licensed or approved by an authorized non-Indian licensing agency; and as a final option, the child is to be placed in an institution approved by the child's tribe or operated by an Indian organization which has a program suitable to meet the Indian child's needs. The preferencing provisions may be overridden if there is "good cause." ICWA, however, does not define "good cause" and state courts have found "good cause" under a variety of circumstances.

- ICWA requires that a removal of an Indian child from her family must be demonstrated by "clear and convincing evidence" that there is the likeliood that serious emotional or physical damage to the child would result if the child were to remain in the home and that "active efforts" were made to keep the family together. Termination of parental rights must be supported by evidence, "including testimony of expert witnesses," that demonstrates "beyond a reasonable doubt" that continued custody of the child by the parent or Indian custodian is likely to result in serious emotional or physical damage to the child [§1912].

The key procedural provisions relate to tribal court jurisdiction. Indian tribes, unlike other cultural communities in the U.S., hold a unique political and legal status, including the power to create and implement their own court systems to adjudicate a range of issues, including child welfare and child custody matters [Carleton 1997; Risling 1998]. Although Indian tribal governments have enjoyed self-governing capacity and limited sovereignty and since the 1960s have been more actively involved with the administration of social services [Mannes 1990], ICWA recognized that state and county child welfare agencies often ignored tribal authorities or refused to follow tribal court directives regarding foster care and adoptive placements of Indian children. ICWA thus expressly recognized the jurisdiction of tribal courts to adjudicate child custody proceedings [§ 1911], delineating tribal jurisdictional powers in two cases:

- First, if an Indian child is domiciled or residing on a reservation, the tribal court has exclusive jurisdiction. Exclusive jurisdiction in these cases resides with the tribal court, however, only in those states not covered by P.L. 280 under which state courts in designated states have concurrent jurisdiction over child welfare matters involving Indian families [Thorne 1999].

- Second, if an Indian child is not domiciled or residing on a reservation, the tribal court has concurrent jurisdiction with the State, and a case involving foster care placement and adoption should be transferred, absent good cause, to the tribal court upon petition by the child's parent, Indian custodian, or tribe.

Tribes are entitled to notice of any involuntary proceeding involving the foster care placement of or termination of parental rights to an Indian child [§ 1912]. Additionally, tribes have the right to petition to invalidate state court determinations made in contravention of the provisions of ICWA that govern tribal court jurisdiction, notice to tribes, and the taking of voluntary consents to foster care placements or termination of parental rights [§ 1914].

Culture and the "Best Interests" of the Child, Tribal Interests, and Parents' Rights

Two interrelated themes in the many analyses of ICWA by lawyers, social workers, and other commentators are the concept of "best interests" of the child, as traditionally understood and applied and as conceptualized under ICWA, and the role that culture should or should not play in the adoption of Indian children. Consideration related to children's "best interests" are often intertwined with issues related to the rights of Indian parents and the interests of the tribes.

The Concept of "Best Interests" in ICWA

Many commentators maintain that ICWA codifies the "best interests" of the child standard traditionally applied by courts and child welfare practitioners in making adoption and other child custody decisions. They interpret ICWA as dispensing with individualized determinations of a child's "best interests" typically made by courts and, for Indian children, expressly mandating that "best interests" lie in sustaining the Indian child's cultural identity through continued involvement with his heritage and his tribe [Bennett 1993; Carleton 1997].

Others, however, maintain that ICWA, while placing emphasis on the cultural heritage and tribal connections of Indian children, nevertheless allows discretion by courts in determining the "best interests" of an individual child [Thorne 1999]. Thorne [1999], for example, disputes the interpretation of ICWA as creating a "cookie cutter" approach to "best interests" of an Indian child, arguing that ICWA mandates a process for state court decision-making regarding foster care placements and adoption for Indian children, and not a specified result.

State courts that have applied the express provisions of ICWA have recognized that an important aspect of an Indian child's "best interests" is the child's connection to the tribe, holding that through ICWA, "Congress sought to protect the interests of Indian tribes and communities and the interests of the Indian children themselves" [*In re Adoption of T.N.F.* 1989]; that ICWA is "based on the interest the tribe has in its children" [*In the matter of Baby Boy Doe* 1993]; that consideration must be given "not only to the wishes of the parents, but the well-being and interests of the child and the tribe" [*In the Adoption of Lindsay C.* 1991]; and that "under ICWA, what is best for an Indian child is to maintain ties with the Indian tribe, culture, and family" [*Yavapai-Apache v. Mejia* 1995, p. 169]. Goldsmith [1995, p. 4] suggests, in line with these courts' holdings, that ICWA presumes that: "[I]t is in the best interest of an Indian child that the role of the tribal community in the child's life be protected. Thus, the dual purposes promoted by the Act—the 'best interests of Indian children' and the promotion of 'stability and security of Indian tribes and families'—are intertwined."

Risling [1998, p. 67] similarly observes that this intertwining of interests was designed "to assure that cultural bias and misunderstanding do not adversely impact an Indian child's relationship with his or her Indian family and tribe." As these American Indian commentators suggest, ICWA's intertwining of children's, families,' and tribal interests is consistent with Indian cultural traditions, which view children as belonging to the family and to the tribe [Brooks 1994]. The integration of the interests of children, families, and tribes is also consistent with the "collective rights" thinking and community values that characterize many Indian tribes [Carleton 1997, p. 38], a paradigm in which the individual is viewed as part of the broader cultural group.

The cultural and legal integration of the interests of Indian children, family, and tribe and the broad definition of "family" to include extended family members and other adults of the tribe have given rise to significant controversy. The conflict may arise because these approaches are at odds with European American social and legal constructs that emphasize individualism, individual rights, rights of the nuclear family, and exclusivity in parent-child relationships [Carriere 1994]. The social and legal system that is based on these European American values differs in fundamental ways from Indian cultural traditions. From the social perspective, Cross [1986, p. 285] notes that historically, the traditions of Indian culture protected children "in a society in which child-rearing was a community affair, in which behavioral expectations and discipline were clearly structured and in which children were highly valued." From the legal perspective, Brooks [1994, p. 665] writes:

> In devising a system of child placement and adoption designed to distance the child from his or her biological family, American jurisprudence has created a system of child rearing that is foreign to the American Indian population, upon which the process is used disproportionately. Often, tribal languages do not have an analog for the Anglo word "adoption." Equally unknown to American Indian culture is the characteristic termination of all ties with an original family in order to create a new set of attachments with a separate family. The spiritual bonds between mother and child, father and child, child and family, as acknowledged in native peoples' cultural beliefs, make severance incomprehensible.

The decision of a Navajo District Court in *In re J.J.S.* [1983], a case in which the court approved the adoption of a child by a member of the child's extended family, highlights the differences between Navajo child rearing practices and European American social and legal traditions. The tribal judge noted that the care of Navajo children was not the exclusive responsibility of parents but was shared by extended family and further commented that:

> Anglo-European law is primarily concerned with the immediate parent and child relationship while Navajo Law is concerned with the relationship of a child to a group which shares the expectation that its members will take care of each other's children [1983, p. 6032].

Some commentators have argued that ICWA's integration of child, family, and tribal interests is unworkable, if not affirmatively harmful. Some contend that the Act, in fact, creates a hierarchy of interests that in effect undermines any genuine consideration of the child's interests. Hollinger [1989, p. 456], for example, argues that ICWA directs that "tribal governing bodies, not parents, should determine the circumstances in which Indian children will be raised." Fischler [1980] contends that the Act places too much weight on the combined rights of parents and tribes at the expense of children's rights to safety.

Other commentators, however, strongly disagree with such interpretations of ICWA. Thorne [1999], for example, emphasizes the discretion of state courts to invoke "good cause" in the individual interests of children. His analysis of ICWA acknowledges that the Act demands greater rigor on the part of state courts because of their history of excessive and arbitrary removals of Indian children from their families and tribes. ICWA, for example, requires that state courts rely on "qualified experts" with knowledge of Indian social and cultural standards to establish that continued custody would likely result in serious emotional or physical harm to the child [§ 1912; see Risling 1998, p. 9]. Even with the more stringent requirements of ICWA, however, he maintains that state courts have broad discretion to address the needs of an individual child. Through a finding of "good cause," state courts may decline to transfer a case to a tribal court when there is concurrent jurisdiction, and through a finding of "good cause," state courts may decline to follow the "preferencing section" of ICWA [Thorne 1999; see Risling 1998]. Thorne also makes the point that exclusive jurisdiction with a tribal court does not mean an absence of attention to the individual needs of a child whose interests are to be determined by that court. To the contrary, he notes that these courts are closest to the children and families whose interests they are determining and have first-hand knowledge of the standards of the Indian community. From his perspective, concerns that individual children's "best interests" are disregarded under ICWA or that there is an undue emphasis on tribal authority are misplaced.

"Best Interests" in Relation to Tribal Interests and Cultural Connections

One of the underpinnings of ICWA that has given rise to substantial debate is the Act's recognition of the interests of the tribes and the Act's explicit response to concerns regarding the survival of Indian culture. The Act states that children are vital to the "continued existence and integrity of Indian tribes" [§1901] and, to that end, it focuses on cultural survival through ensuring the continuation of Indian children's connections with their tribes. Watts [1989, p. 213] writes that "the steady flow of a disproportionately high percentage of Indian children from their families and tribes to non-Indian foster and adoptive homes and institutions threaten[ed] to deprive tribes of the most basic necessity for their survival—a next generation." Mannes [1993, p. 143] describes these practices as posing the threat of "cultural genocide." It is clear that ICWA recognized the critical need to ensure the survival of Indian culture. As Blanchard and Barsh [1980, p. 354] write:

> With enactment of the Indian Child Welfare Act, the federal government responded affirmatively to the petition of American Indians that their way of life be allowed

to continue. At issue is not tribal rights versus individual rights, but rather the right of a people to maintain a culture that has provided them meaning in this world from the beginning of time.

ICWA's focus on the continued survival of Indian tribes, however, has been criticized by those who contend that the Act does not permit any individualized determination of Indian children's "best interests." The argument, in essence, is that a child's best interests may not always coincide with a culture's right to survival or with values associated with the child's being brought up in and deriving identity from her culture of origin [MacEachron et al. 1996]. Critics insist that ICWA is inherently flawed because the Act definitively equates each Indian child's culture and tribal connections with "best interests" and places overarching emphasis on the continued viability of a culture [Bakeis 1996, p. 543]. Bennett [1993], who also argues that ICWA mandates predetermined results for Indian children, questions the very legitimacy of tribal interests in children, writing that "the concerns of American Indian tribes and the widespread break-up of American Indian families does not mean that children should be used to further a social policy at their own expense" [1993, pp. 969–970]. The "social policy" of ICWA to which she presumably refers—which is directed to halting the disintegration of families and tribes and the promotion of efforts to preserve Indian family and culture—may be, however, difficult to view as an experiment under which the welfare of Indian children is sacrificed, particularly in light of the impact of earlier social policies on the psychological development and well-being of Indian children.

Bakeis [1996], in a similar vein, argues that ICWA works against children's "best interests" through its emphasis on preservation of a child's ties to family and tribe. She takes specific issue with ICWA's requirements of a heightened burden of proof for removing children from their families (clear and convincing evidence) and for termination of parental rights (beyond a reasonable doubt), asserting that these provisions discriminate against Indian children. She contends that ICWA "potentially [forces] children who lack ties with traditional Indian society to experience more abuse and neglect before the state can take action on their behalf" and requires them "to remain in a state of parentless limbo longer than other children in the same situation" [Bakeis 1996, p. 553]. These emotionally-charged arguments ignore both the rapidity with which Indian children historically were removed from their families and the realities of the foster care system, in which both Indian and non-Indian children alike maintain their legal relationships to their birth parents and do not, at any point short of termination of parental rights, become even briefly "parentless." They may raise more legitimate concerns regarding the protection of children, though the extent to which a child may be at greater risk as a result of a higher burden of proof to justify removal from her family is, even in Bakeis' words, a potentiality.

Bakeis also argues that there is little or no basis for concluding that non-Indian placements of Indian children work against Indian children's "best interests." Expressing skepticism that placement of Indian children in non-Indian homes results in any psychological harm to Indian children, she relies on Bartholet's conclusions [1991, p. 1209] regarding the "astounding uniformity" of the research showing that transracial adoption is "working well from the viewpoint of the children and the adoptive families"—research that has studied outcomes for African American children adopted as infants and not Indian children removed from their families and tribes. Bakeis nonetheless concludes that this research is equally applicable to Indian children and maintains that any potential harm to Indian children in transcultural adoptive placements is "speculative at best" [1996, p. 548].

The research, although somewhat limited, is sufficient, however, to demonstrate that Indian children placed with non-Indian adoptive families are at risk in relation to overall well-being and identity. Fanshel's early research [1972] on outcomes for Indian children adopted by Caucasian families, although generally indicating positive outcomes in terms of the children's physical and emotional status, revealed potential problems in the areas of personality and behavior. Fanshel [1972, pp. 322–323] wrote that:

My overall impression is that the children are doing remarkably well as a group. From a physical growth and developmental standpoint, they appear to be thriving ... In the realm of personality and behavior patterns there are more incipient signs of difficulty than in other areas, but this is true of only thirty percent of the children and most of these are seen to have moderate rather than serious problems.

Fanshel's finding that almost one-third of the Indian children were experiencing "moderate" problems in the areas of personality development and behavior may undermine his more optimistic assessment that these children were doing "remarkably well." Fanshel did acknowledge that Indian children adopted by non-Indians were at greater risk in adolescence, a concern frequently raised by clinicians and researchers. Roll [1986, cited in Matheson 1996, p. 233], for example, writes that:

Cross-racial adoptions (often) and cross racial Indian adoptions (almost always) have a high likelihood of producing severe identity crisis in Indian children as those children become adolescents. The children thus raised are at more serious risk for depression, suicide, anti-social behavior, severe identity crisis. In addition to the problems within the Indian child raised in non-Indian homes, there are also problems of social interaction (prejudice) which make the risk of psychological difficulties (isolation and displacement) in the Indian child even higher.

Social scientists [Fischler 1980; Guerrero 1979] have associated the high suicide rate among Indian adolescents, approximately twice the national average, with rearing out of Indian culture. Villanueva [1990], in his review of the data regarding psychological disorders among Indian adolescents who have been transculturally adopted, found that transculturally placed Indian adolescents are at much higher risk for psychological disorders and destructive behaviors, including suicide, when they enter young adulthood. These outcomes appear to be associated with a psychological process by which Indian young people identify with the aggressor—"white" society—a process associated with a lack of contemporary Indian role models and involving, for many Indian children, an intense level of self-hatred [Thorne 1999].

Westermeyer [1974] described the identity confusion of Indian children raised in non-Indian families as the "Apple Syndrome," in which the child is American Indian by heritage but embraces a cultural identity that is "white." He found that children with a sense of cultural confusion struggle with personal and social identity and experience higher rates of status offenses and a greater prevalence of emotional problems. In his testimony before the U.S. Senate four years before ICWA was enacted, he stated that Indian children who grew up in wholly Caucasian environments:

> [These children] were raised with a white cultural and social identity. They were raised in a white home. They attended predominantly white schools . . . and really came to understand very little about Indian culture, Indian behavior, and had virtually no viable Indian identity. They can recall such things as seeing cowboys and Indians on TV and feeling that Indians were a historical figure but were not a viable contemporary social group. Then during adolescence, they found that society was not to grant them the white identity that they had. . . For example, a universal experience was that when they began to date white children, the parents of the white youngsters were against this, and there were pressures among white children from these parents not to date these Indian children [Westermeyer 1974].

He concluded that "society was putting on [Indian children] an identity which they didn't possess and taking from them an identity they did possess" [Westermeyer 1974]. American Indian adults adopted as children by non-Indian families frequently report, however, that Indian identity was not an identity they could even "possess" because of the absence of any opportunity to connect with their Indian heritage during childhood or adolescence [Thorne 1999; see Westermeyer 1979].

Indian Parents' Rights and ICWA

A criticism of ICWA that also surfaces in some of the commentaries about the Act is that it violates the rights of Indian birth parents who wish to voluntarily place their children for adoption and whose rights to do so are inappropriately limited by the Act. Bakeis [1996], for example, contends that ICWA violates birth parents' rights in two ways. First, she argues that ICWA deprives Indian parents of the opportunity to personally select the adoptive parents for their child, which she asserts is "everyone else's right" [Bakeis 1996, p. 563]. It is well established that the rights of birth parents—Indian and non-Indian—do not extend to an absolute privilege to choose the adoptive parents for their children [Sussman & Guggenheim 1980], and in fact, birth parent selection of adoptive parents is an adoption practice that has only recently been implemented to any extent [Modell 1994]. This practice reflects a range of considerations related to greater openness in adoption and an acknowledgment of the benefits of involving birth parents in making such a choice, but the practice is not based on a legal "right."

Second, Bakeis asserts that ICWA violates birth parents' "right of anonymity" by requiring tribal involvement, a right which she claims is legally cognizable and "permits birth mothers and fathers to remain anonymous until the child turns eighteen" [1996, p. 566]. This misstatement of the law suggests special harm to Indian birth parents as a result of ICWA. Contrary to her assertion, current law in most states maintains the identity of birth parents as permanently confidential information even as to their children, a legal practice criticized by birth parents, adoptees, and adoptive parents alike [Dusky 1996; Feigelman & Silverman 1986]. As a consequence, the identities of all birth parents are maintained in sealed records and not released when the adoptee reaches the age of majority. Second, ICWA, in reality, provides Indian adoptees with greater access to information than state laws typically provide other adoptees. ICWA provides that "an Indian individual who has reached the age of eighteen and who was the subject of an adoptive placement" may apply to the court that granted the final adoption decree and obtain information regarding the "tribal

affiliation, if any, of the individual's biological parents and provide such other information as may be necessary to protect any
rights flowing from the individual's tribal heritage" [§1917]. This
provision, if implemented as written, would in fact maintain
adoption information under seal but release it to an adult Indian
adoptee at the age of eighteen—the very "right" that Bakeis claims
is provided to non-Indians but not to Indian adoptees and birth
families. Despite this provision in ICWA, however, it appears that
such informational access is not a reality [Edwards 1999]. Information often is not available to Indian adoptees to permit them to
locate the appropriate court of jurisdiction [Thorne 1999], and
even when the appropriate court is determined, courts rarely
approve the applications of Indian adoptees for such information
[Edwards 1999]. Consequently, Indian adoptees face the same
challenges in obtaining information on their birth families as do
non-Indian adoptees, a reality that impacts equivalently on the
interests of birth parents.

In summary, ICWA views the interests of Indian children,
parents, and tribes as closely associated with cultural identity.
The arguments against a focus on cultural considerations have
tended to cast ICWA as extending inadequate protections to
children, a view that may, in reality, more closely reflect, in the
words of one court, "Anglo cultural biases" [*Yavapai-Apache v.
Mejia* 1995, p. 169]. The integration of individual, family, and
tribal interests is at variance from European American cultural
and legal constructs and has given rise to considerable tension
over the meaning of "best interests" for Indian children. The
differing views of Indian and non-Indian commentators is a telling
commentary on the cultural, social, and legal divide which generally exists between Indian and non-Indian communities.

Who is "Indian"?

An argument also made in criticism of ICWA is that the status of
"Indian" child should be defined narrowly so that only certain
children of Indian heritage are within the requirements of the Act.
This argument, in essence, holds that unless a child is "Indian

enough" genetically and socially, ICWA and its rigorous protections should not apply. Bakeis [1996, p. 558], for example, who takes issue with the Act's focus on "blood ties or race of the child," maintains that whether a child is "Indian" should be determined on a combination of biological factors—such as "the appropriate amount of Indian blood"—and social factors—such as whether the child is living with an Indian parent and whether the child is living or has lived on a reservation or in "an Indian community." Her ill-defined construct of an "appropriate amount of Indian blood"—a standard specifically defined and used by some Indian tribes but not by all in determining who is a tribal member [Thorne 1999]—may, in reality, go more to the issue of who should make the determination of who is "Indian," with the implication that a uniform blood quantum standard regarding Indian heritage be established by some authority other than the tribes. The social factors that she would mandate to establish "Indian" status raise fundamental questions regarding the meaningfulness of cultural heritage. Does a culture "matter" to an individual, for example, only to the extent of direct and personal experience with that culture? Are cultural and tribal connections important to a child only if his or her parents live a "traditional" Indian life? And to what extent should genetic and social tests of being "Indian"— individually or jointly—be imposed? Bakeis [1996, p. 585] would seem to suggest that even if a child's American Indian heritage is of sufficient genetic magnitude, irrespective of how that standard is defined and by whom, the child is "Indian enough" only if she lives on a reservation or in a "traditional Indian home."

A common approach to avoiding the application of ICWA is the contention that a child and/or his or her birth parents do not have sufficient ties to an Indian tribe as to warrant the protections of the Act. The essence of this position, which is similar to the argument that a child must be "Indian enough," is that ICWA should apply only when the child is a member of an "existing Indian family," with direct connections to Indian culture, and the Act should not apply when there is no "existing Indian family" from which a child is being removed [Gallagher 1994]. In the period before the U.S. Supreme Court's ruling in *Mississippi Band of Choctaw Indians v. Holyfield* [1989] (discussed below), courts largely were persuaded by this argument. In *In re Adoption of Baby Boy L.* [1982], for example, the court considered the case of an unwed Indian father who was enrolled as a member of his tribe and was incarcerated at the time of his child's birth and a non-Indian birth mother who voluntarily placed her child for adoption without complying with ICWA. The court held that the Act should not apply because the case involved "an illegitimate infant who has never been a member of an Indian home or culture, and probably never would be" [1982, p. 175]. In *In re Adoption of T.R.M.* [1988], an Indian birth mother consented to the adoption of her child when the child was five days old, without compliance with ICWA, and then, within a year, sought the assistance of her tribe in regaining custody of her child. After seven years of proceedings, the court upheld the adoption on the basis that the child had never been part of an Indian family, except for her first five days of life— an analysis suggesting that because the child had spent her life with an non-Indian family over the course of protracted litigation, her Indian heritage was not relevant [Davis 1993]. Not all courts prior to the *Holyfield* decision, however, recognized the "existing Indian family" exception to ICWA. The New Jersey Supreme Court, in *In re Adoption of a Child of Indian Heritage* [1988, p. 932], for example, held that:

> While an unwed mother might have a legitimate and genuine interest in placing her child for adoption outside of an Indian environment, if she believes that such a placement is in the child's best interests, consideration must also be given to the rights of the child's father and Congress' belief that, whenever possible, it is in an Indian child's best interests to maintain a relationship with his or her tribe.

The pivotal court decision regarding the issue of "Indian" status for purposes of application of ICWA is the U.S. Supreme Court's holding in *Mississippi Band of Choctaw Indians v. Holyfield* [1989], a case involving a dispute regarding tribal jurisdiction over the adoption of children of Indian parents born off the reservation. In *Holyfield*, the unmarried Indian mother and father left the reservation shortly before the mother gave birth to twins. The birth parents consented to adoption of the twins by a non-Indian family, a decision to which the tribe objected and over which it claimed jurisdiction. The state court ruled, and the Supreme Court of Mississippi agreed, that the tribe did not have exclusive jurisdiction under ICWA because the children had been born off the reservation and neither of the newborns had ever physically lived there. The U.S. Supreme Court reversed the decision of the Mississippi Supreme Court.

One key aspect of the U.S. Supreme Court's decision was its recognition that ICWA was "not solely about the interests of Indian children and families, but also about the impact on the tribes themselves of the large numbers of Indian children adopted by non-Indians" [*Mississippi* 1989, p. 49]. Clarifying that tribal jurisdiction was "not meant to be defeated by the actions of individual members of the tribe," the Court held that "the protection of this tribal interest is at the core of ICWA, which recognizes that the tribe has an interest in the child which is distinct from but on a parity with the interest of parents" [1989, p. 49].

Equally important, the Court focused on the status of the children as Indian. Citing the decision by the Supreme Court of Utah in *In re Adoption of Halloway*, the Court noted that:

> This relationship between Indian tribes and Indian children domiciled on the reservation finds no parallel in other ethnic cultures found in the United States. It is a relationship that many non-Indians find difficult to understand and that non-Indian courts are slow to recognize. [*Mississippi* 1989, p. 52]

The Court, rejecting the contention that the children lacked a sufficient connection to their Indian heritage by virtue of their birth off the reservation, concluded that on "the legal question of *who* should make the custody determination" concerning the twins, ICWA placed "the decision in the hands of the Choctaw

Tribal Court," and the Court deferred to the "experience, wisdom, and compassion" of that court [1989, p. 53–54]. Commenting on the course of this particular litigation, the Court further observed:

> Had the mandate of the ICWA been followed in 1986 [when the twins were placed for adoption] ... much potential anguish might have been avoided, and in any case the law cannot be applied so as to automatically "reward those who obtain custody, whether lawfully or otherwise, and maintain it during any ensuing (and protracted) litigation" (Citing *In re Adoption of Halloway*) [1989, p. 54].

It is of note that upon assuming jurisdiction of the case, the Choctaw Tribal Court permitted the adoption of the twins by the non-Indian family [Bennett 1993]. That outcome, in line with Thorne's analysis of ICWA [1999], suggests that the tribal court paid close attention to the individualized "best interests" of the children in determining their ultimate custody.

Since *Holyfield*, courts may be more strictly interpreting ICWA and more consistently applying the Act when Indian children have not been raised by parents with demonstrably significant ties to a reservation or an Indian cultural environment [Gallagher 1994]. The Oregon Court of Appeals, for example, in *Quinn v. Walters* [1993, p. 206] rejected the attempted reliance on the "Indian family" exception, writing that "if ICWA does not apply because the parent is not 'Indian' enough for a particular state court, the protection afforded to the child, the parents, and the tribe is defeated."

The issue of who is an "Indian child" or an "Indian family," however, remains a matter of dispute. Some argue that a child's genetic Indian heritage should not be determinative of birth parents' ability to voluntarily place their children for adoption without tribal involvement. Hollinger [n.d.], for example, asks with regard to Indian children:

> To what extent should the destiny of children be deter-mined by their racial or genetic heritage, their affiliation

with various ethnic, cultural or tribal communities, their birth parents' voluntary placement decisions, or when they grow up, their own choices concerning their individual or group identities?

She points with approval to the case of *Bridget R. v. Cindy R.* [1996] in which the California appellate court ruled that unless a child is part of a clearly identifiable Indian family—that is, a family in which one or both birth parents have a "significant social, cultural, or political relationship" with a federally recognized tribe— ICWA should not apply. Hollinger places great weight on the interests of the newly constituted adoptive family, writing that "although the interest in not breaking up a genuine Indian family is arguably compelling, an interest in interfering with an adoptive placement of a child who was never part of an existing Indian family is clearly not compelling." She maintains that:

> [C]hildren have equal protection rights to *not* be classified on the basis of blood alone and to *not* be "protected" against adoptive placements that pose no threat to their sociocultural identity. Children also have rights *not* to be retroactively claimed as Indian tribal members simply for the purpose of challenging an otherwise valid adoption under state law [emphasis in original].

Her conclusions suggest a concern that tribes arbitrarily claim any and all potential members, an assumption that Thorne [1999] argues is neither socially nor economically desirable from the tribal perspective. Hollinger, however, maintains that tribal survival is the overriding motivation that prompts tribes to claim "current and future generations of children of partial Indian descent whose initial tribal ties may be nonexistent or quite attenuated," and whose immediate families "have grown apart from or actively disavowed tribal culture."

The ongoing controversy regarding who is an "Indian" child and who constitutes an "Indian" family surfaced legislatively in 1995 when amendments were introduced to "clarify" ICWA by more narrowly defining an "Indian child" in relation to membership in a tribe. The "Pryce Amendment," introduced by three members of the U.S. House of Representatives, including Representative Deborah Pryce of Ohio [1995], would have deleted from current law the definition of an "Indian child" as a child "eligible for membership" in an Indian tribe [§ 1903(4)(b)] and limited the status of an "Indian" child to "only those who are on the membership roll of a tribe or those who are otherwise considered members under consistently applied policies and practices, and in accordance with all written requirements for membership."

The stated purpose of this proposed change in the law, which mirrors and attempts to codify in federal law the "Indian family" exception [Carleton 1997], was two-fold: to prevent birth parents who "had absolutely no affiliation with a tribe either before, or at the time of the child's birth" from "arbitrarily" and "retroactively" designating themselves as members of an Indian tribe; and to disallow tribes in these circumstances from attempting to invoke the protections afforded by ICWA in an effort to affect the outcome of adoptive placements [Pryce 1995].

Opposition to this amendment immediately surfaced from the American Indian community as it was viewed as "conditioning the definition of an 'Indian child' upon the formal enrollment of the biological parent as members of a tribe at the time of the child's birth" [Gray Eyes 1995] and "violat[ing] the right of a tribe to determine its own membership," particularly given the fact that "enrollment lists" are not "a traditional practice of tribes, but rather have been foisted upon tribes by the federal government" [Cross 1995]. On the other side of the debate, some adoption agencies and private adoption attorneys fully supported the amendment, viewing it as more compatible with traditional concepts of "best interests" of the child [Carleton 1997]. Alternative amendments were subsequently proposed by American Indian groups, but no action had been taken as of Spring 2000 either on the Pryce Amendment or subsequent proposed amendments.

The goals of the Pryce Amendment raise a number of questions, including issues related to the primary interests served by the proposed changes to ICWA. Do these goals reflect overarching concerns that children are being harmed by the preferencing section of ICWA that places value on children being raised by Indian families? Or is the primary concern that the law places too many constraints on the ability of non-Indians to adopt Indian children?

A theme that surfaces in the pre-ICWA history of child welfare practice is the extent to which decisions to remove Indian children from their families and communities was tied to a desire to meet the demands of Caucasians for infants to adopt. One commentator, for example, has written that judicial support of social workers' decisions to remove Indian children from their families "encourage[d] unscrupulous welfare workers seeking to find adoptable children to combat the perceived shortage" of children available for adoption [Gallagher 1994, p. 86]. Joseph Reid, director of the Child Welfare League of America in the 1970s, wrote in the forward to Fanshel's research [1972] that a significant motivation behind states' efforts to place Indian children with Caucasian families was a desire to meet the interests of Caucasians in adopting. The same goal may be connected with strategies reportedly used by those seeking to adopt Indian children—including encouraging American Indian birth parents to keep silent regarding their child's heritage or to renounce their Indian tribal membership and assisting Indian parents to move children out of the country beyond the jurisdiction of federal law [see Risling 1998].

The number of adoptive placements of Caucasian infants has declined even more significantly since the 1970s as a result of legalization of abortion, greater access to birth control, and changing social attitudes regarding unmarried parenting [Mosher & Bachrach 1996]. At the same time, the demand to adopt among Caucasian women has grown as a result of increasing rates of infertility and delayed childbearing patterns [Mosher & Bachrach 1996]. In this demographic and social environment, the forces leading to the Pryce Amendment may likewise involve considerations that mirror the role adoption demand played in the 1970s with regard to decisions to place Indian children with non-Indian families. The provisions appear to place great weight on protecting the viability of adoptive placements of Indian children, presumably infants rather than older children removed from their families and tribes, against the "arbitrary" behavior of Indian birth parents and tribal authorities in reclaiming their children. The Pryce Amendment may reflect some of the same concerns regarding the rights of prospective Caucasian adoptive parents that led to the enactment of MEPA, particularly in an environment in which the availability of Caucasian infants for adoption is limited and there is increasing interest in adopting children from other racial and cultural groups.

The Effectiveness of ICWA

It is difficult to draw conclusions regarding the overall effectiveness of ICWA since its enactment more than twenty years ago because published data on foster care placements and adoption rates of Indian children are lacking. Studies conducted for the period 1975–1986 indicated that ICWA significantly decreased the number of adoptions of Indian children and more moderately decreased state foster care placements of Indian children [MacEachron et al. 1996]. Those studies indicated that the average state adoption rate for Indian children had become roughly comparable to that of non-Indian children whereas it had previously been three times higher. Data also indicated that state foster care placement rates for Indian children were reduced, but they remained three times higher than the foster care placement rate for non-Indian children [MacEachron et al. 1996].

Subsequent studies have pointed to a range of issues bearing on the effectiveness of ICWA. A 1984 study by the California Department of Social Services, for example, found widespread failures to comply with the procedural provisions of ICWA, with county social workers and adoption agencies failing to notify tribes in 80% of the voluntary placements of Indian infants [Smith 1988]. The Department noted considerable resistance to ICWA by both agency staff and adoption attorneys who viewed ICWA compliance merely as added paperwork that extended the adoption process by a year or more [Smith 1988]. McCarthy's study of the implementation of ICWA in Idaho [1993] found that ICWA had not substantially reduced the number of Indian children placed in foster care or with adoptive families. He did find, however, that there had been an increase in the percentage of Indian children placed in homes in which at least one parent was Indian, although the placements made by the state agency, as opposed to tribal authorities, continued to involve few Indian homes [McCarthy 1993].

The most comprehensive study of the impact of ICWA, commissioned by the Administration of Children, Youth, and Families of the U.S. Department of Human Services and the Bureau of Indian Affairs, was conducted in 1985 [Plantz et al. 1988]. That study showed that although public agencies and state courts were in many instances complying with certain provisions of ICWA, there was a continuing excessive placement of Indian children in foster care at a rate 3.6 times greater than the general population. The researchers found that foster care placements of Indian children, in fact, had increased by one-quarter since the enactment of ICWA, rising from 7,200 children in the early 1980s to approximately 9,000 in 1986. The report, however, indicated that notification of Indian families and tribes in cases of involuntary child placements had improved dramatically. The percentage of Indian parents who received notice that the family was at risk that their child may be involuntarily removed from their home rose from near zero before 1978 to 65%–70% after passage of the Act, and notice to tribes in these instances reached 80%. Improvements were also noted in the number of relative placements for Indian children removed from the custody of their birth parents, with 47% of the children placed with extended family. Children placed by state agencies, nonetheless, were found to stay in out-of-home care longer than Caucasian children and to be placed in more restrictive settings.

The view of many commentators is that the removal of Indian children from their families and tribes and the placement of Indian children with non-Indian families continues at an excessive rate [Carleton 1997; Watts 1989; Edwards 1999]. A number of courts have avoided applying ICWA, ignoring the substantive provisions of the law, assuming jurisdiction in cases in which tribal courts have concurrent or exclusive jurisdiction, or engrafting exceptions to ICWA that are not included in the law [Watts 1989]. Gallagher [1994, p. 105] states that no definitive statement can be made about ICWA's success or failure because it has been "susceptible to incompatible interpretations by each court" in the 50 states. In large part, there has been among courts a "failure to recognize that the best interests of Indian children may not necessarily mirror those of children in mainstream America" [Gallagher 1994, p. 105]. Similarly, Watts [1989, p. 250] notes the challenges to the judicial system posed by ICWA:

> It is inherently difficult for a system founded on individual rights to deal effectively with a cultural system based on communal duties and responsibilities and in which individual rights are subordinate to the good of the group. The rights of communities are generally secondary to the rights of individuals in contemporary American society and it is a philosophical leap for courts to reverse this thought process when dealing with Indian tribes. Indeed, although it may be valid to question whether two such diametrically opposite views of rights can or should coexist for any substantial period of time, ICWA does in fact encourage the existence of the tribal communal culture and requires the non-Indian legal system to recognize and accommodate it.

Because many state courts continue to "fail to consider the cultural identity of the children with whom they are dealing," there is concern that Indian families continue to be at risk of separation, Indian children continue to face "cultural confusion and disorientation" because of placement in non-Indian homes[Watts 1989, p. 215], and adoptive families continue to face the possibility that their adoptions will not be finalized because courts have failed to comply with ICWA.

Kunesh [1996] goes beyond judicial factors in analyzing the limited success of ICWA in decreasing the number of placements of Indian children in foster care and the number of adoptive placements with non-Indian families. She identifies the external forces of "discrimination and destruction of tribal and family interests" that have resulted from federal and state government action [1996, p. 18]. In addition, however, she identifies the problem that "occurs when a tribe loses sight of tribal or individual Indian rights and fails to assert its tribal sovereignty to protect these vital interests" [1996, p. 18]. She writes that:

> Tribes must begin to heed the warning signs of a potentially self-destructive internal upheaval of Indian families and children, and begin to address the reasons for this alarming development—reasons which are due, in no small measure, to the failure of tribes to fully exercise their tribal sovereignty [1996, p. 19].

She focuses on the poverty, powerlessness, cultural disorientation, and substance abuse that plague "every layer of American Indians' lives and culture" [1996, p. 30]. These factors, as borne out by a recent study by the University of Iowa [1993], have been key reasons that placements of Indian children in foster care have persisted at disproportionately high levels. Kunesh [1996] urges the integral involvement of tribes in all Indian child welfare matters and the development of tribally based programs for Indian children and families that meet the needs of the tribal community through a continuum of services.

Transcultural Placements

A final consideration relating to the role of culture in the adoption of American Indian children is presented by cases in which Indian families are not available for the foster care of Indian children or as adoptive resources for Indian children who cannot be reared by their birth parents or extended tribal family. A non-Indian adoptive placement may be necessary because of an established long-term relationship between the child and family, a dearth of adequately funded tribal child welfare services, or remoteness of the reservation [Watts 1989]. When non-Indian placements are necessary, Watts [1989, p. 253] emphasizes that "in making an interracial placement decision, courts must recognize and attempt to address the potential problems the adopted children, their adoptive families, and their tribe are likely to face." Similarly, child welfare agencies must be aware of the issues related to cultural identity as they affect Indian children, birth and adoptive families, and tribes. The work done by such groups as The Native American Children and Family Services (NACFS) Institute highlights the issues that are critical to an understanding of American Indian culture in foster care placements and adoption. The NACFS curriculum [n.d.], for example, focuses on the traditions and cultures of Indian people as well as the issues related to attachment and loss, intergenerational grief, the effects of addiction on children, and permanency outcomes.

The resolution of the issues involved in non-Indian adoptive placements of Indian children may be a complex undertaking. An example of one approach is that taken by a Navajo tribal court which, when the child's extended family and the tribe contested an adoption to which the Indian birth mother had agreed, granted permanent guardianship to the family who sought to adopt; allowed the birth mother to retain her parental rights; granted the extended birth family "open and liberal" visitation rights; and ensured tribal membership for the child [Watts 1989, p. 253–254]. Recognizing that the social and judicial manageability of such an approach is yet to be determined, Watts [1989] nonetheless points to the benefit of providing a child with a stable and loving family while preserving connections with her cultural heritage and providing a foundation for self-identity.

Summary

The literature on ICWA seems consistent on one point: that the Act is a legislative anomaly. Some commentators view its anomalous nature as positive, reflecting a "community-based policy surrounded by a dominant culture that most values individualism and individual autonomy" and that allows "Indians [to] shape their own culturally sensitive interventions . . . and preserve their unique culture" [MacEachron et al. 1996, p. 460]. Others, however, perceive ICWA in highly negative terms, claiming that it provides inadequate protections to Indian children and in some cases Indian parents—a perspective reflected in the titles of such law review articles as "The Indian Child Welfare Act: Violation of Personal Rights for the Sake of the Tribe" [Bakeis 1996] and "American Indian Children: Caught in the Web of the Indian Child Welfare Act" [Bennett 1993].

Kunesh [1996, p. 32] points out that the "continuing attitude that Indian children are better off if they are raised outside the reservation or Indian communities is still widespread." The historical context leading to the enactment of ICWA reflects the longstanding nature of this perception, and the controversies regarding the scope of ICWA continue to highlight the difficulties which European American social service and legal systems have with the Act's integration of tribal, family, and children's interests. The Act's recognition of the importance of tribal and cultural identity and the role of culture in the adoption of Indian children have generated controversy on the appropriate approach to the "best interests" of Indian children, the definitions of an "Indian child" and Indian family," the rights of Indian parents, and the role of the tribe. Although many perspectives have been brought to bear on this issue, Hodges [1996], the adopted mother of an Indian child, offers the following:

> Before lawmakers encourage adoptions of Indian children by non-Indian families, before they remove tribal jurisdiction over child custody proceedings, before state courts interpret "good cause" as economic superiority, they need to acknowledge that strength of biological and cultural ties that Indian tribes can offer their own children.

Part III

The Role of Race, Culture, and National Origin in International Adoption

By its very nature, international adoption brings into play considerations related to race, culture, and national origin. Questions arise regarding the impact of international adoption on children's racial and cultural identities and their connections with their countries of birth. What should be the role of international adoption in meeting children's needs? Do adoption agencies, adoptive families, and children's adoptive countries have obligations with regard to children's race-, culture- and national origin-based needs when they are internationally adopted? With the growth in international adoption, have the key issues related to race, culture, and national origin been identified and addressed?

Overview

The history of international adoption provides a starting point for a consideration of the role of race, culture, and national origin in the international adoption of children in this country. In the United States, interest in international adoption initially focused on children affected by military conflicts in which the U.S. was involved. The first major wave of international adoption occurred after World War II. A small number of children—approximately 300—were brought to the U.S. through adoption from Poland, Greece, Germany, and Italy [Carro 1995], and a larger number of Asian children were adopted by U.S. families. American families adopted approximately 3,000 children from Japan and 840 children from China between 1948 and 1962 [Weil 1984]. These adoptions came to a virtual end in the 1960s with economic and social developments within Japan and China [Weil 1984]. The next phase of international adoption followed the Korean War. In 1955, Harry Holt, a farmer from Oregon, initiated efforts to ensure that children who had been displaced by the Korean War conflict found adoptive families in the U.S. [Cox 1999]. Federal legislation allowing entry into the U.S. by Korean war orphans and children fathered by U.S. servicemen stationed in Korea further facilitated the adoptions of these children [W.J. Kim 1995]. Later in the 1960s, United States involvement in the Vietnam conflict led to the adoption of several thousand South Vietnamese children by American families [Carro 1995]. As U.S. military involvement drew to a close in the early to mid-1970s, these adoptions declined and then abruptly ceased with the fall of Saigon in 1975 and the controversial "Baby Lift" in April of that year [Cox 1999; Silverman 1993]. With the closure of international adoptions of Vietnamese children, interest turned to Thailand, the Philippines, and India [Cox 1999], countries in which the numbers of international adoptions have varied over time. Since 1993, adoptions of Vietnamese children by U.S. families have resumed and have gradually grown over time (from 110 adoptions in 1993 to 603 adoptions in 1993) [U.S. Department of State 1999].

    Outside of Asia, international adoption of children has been associated, to a large degree, with economic conditions in children's birth countries and a growing acceptance of intercountry adoption as an appropriate alternative for homeless and displaced children. Adoptions of children from Central and South America were relatively rare in the 1950s and 1960s, grew somewhat in the 1970s and 1980s, and then gained more significantly in number in the early 1990s. The number of children adopted from Central and South America by U.S. families in 1998 ranged from a high of 911 children from Guatemala to far smaller numbers of children from other Latin American countries [U.S. Department of State 1999]. Despite the growth in adoptions of Latin American children, however, international adoptions of children from Central and South America have sparked significant debate, fueled to some degree by unsubstantiated rumors that children were being adopted by foreigners for their body parts [Frankel 1995; United States Information Agency 1994]. In Guatemala, in particular, concerns have surfaced that the adoption system in the country, which is largely unregulated and allows independent agents to act as facilitators [Cox 1999], has permitted widespread fraud and corruption [Holt International Families 1999; Ortiz 1998]. The extent to which the international adoptions of Guatemalan children should continue has been questioned [Hester 1999].

International adoptions of children from the Soviet Union were virtually unknown during the "Cold War" era, but with collapse of the communist political system of the Former Soviet Union and the economic crises in its wake, adoptions of children from Russia and Eastern Europe began to grow significantly [Rios-Kohn 1998]. The first wave of adoptions from Eastern Europe occurred in 1989 with the fall of the communist regime in Romania. The world's attention focused on the plight of thousands of children in orphanages, many of whom—though fewer than originally believed—were HIV infected as a result of governmental policies in the 1980s that promoted micro-infusions of blood to underweight infants [McKelvey & Stevens 1994; Perlez 1994]. No system was in place, however, to oversee the international adoptions of Romanian children, and the process became so plagued with problems that Romanian authorities declared a moratorium on international adoption [Wilkinson 1995]. Adoptions were reopened only after the Romanian Adoption Committee was established to oversee all international adoptive placements [Cox 1999]. The number of adoptions of Romanian children by U.S. families reached a high of 2,594 adoptions in 1991, dropped dramatically to 121 adoptions in 1992, and since then, has not exceeded more than about 600 adoptions annually [U.S. Department of State 1999].

By contrast, with the collapse of communism in Russia, the number of international adoptions of Russian children has grown steadily. By 1998, Russia was the country of origin for the largest number of children adopted from other countries by U.S. citizens [U.S. Department of State 1999]. International adoptions of Russian children, however, have not been without controversy. After two high profile incidents involving the adoption of Russian children by U.S. citizens—one involving a couple charged with physically abusing two newly adopted Russian children on the flight home and the other involving the death at the hands of his adoptive mother of a Russian boy diagnosed with reactive attachment disorder—negative sentiment in Russia regarding international adoption ran high [Cummings 1998]. Efforts to place constraints on such adoptions, however, have not had a substantial impact, particularly given the growing number of children in Russian orphanages who cannot be placed with Russian families.

Prior to the mid 1990s, relatively small numbers of Chinese children were adopted by U.S. citizens. Beginning in 1994, however, as China opened its doors more widely to the world, the number of such adoptions began to grow significantly, rising from 787 adoptions in 1994 to 2,130 adoptions in 1995 [U.S. Department of State 1999]. Since that time, China has alternated with Russia as the country from which the largest number of internationally adopted children come to the U.S. Unlike Russia and countries in Eastern Europe, China began its international adoption program with stringent safeguards that ensured close regulation [Cox 1999]. Perhaps because this system was in place from the initiation of the international adoption program, there has been little resistance to international adoption as an alternative for children in orphanages—principally girls without families as a result of the country's one-child-per-family policy and the traditional value placed on males as the offspring who carry on the family line and support their parents in old age [Schoof 1999; Thurston 1996]. China, in fact, revised its laws effective April 1, 1999, to facilitate both domestic and international adoptions of children who are abandoned [Lin 1998].

In contrast to the rapid growth in the number of international adoptions of Russian and Chinese children, the number of intercountry adoptions of children from South Korea by U.S. families has declined. International adoptions have been scaled back significantly by Korea over the past decade [from 8,000 adoptions in 1986 to approximately 1,800 in 1998], at least partially in response to media criticisms of the Korean "export" of abandoned children and a sense of national pride [Cox 1999; Reitman 1999]. Although there has been a long-standing desire to phase out international adoption altogether, the country's recent financial crisis as well as cultural barriers to domestic adoption have worked against the achievement of that goal [Reitman 1999]. Despite efforts to promote domestic adoption, including laws that provide adopted children with the same rights of inheritance as birth children [Cox 1999], adoption has not been well accepted as a result of cultural values associated with the importance of patriarchal bloodlines and a view of adoption as a means of ensuring family continuity rather than providing children with permanent families [W. J. Kim 1995]. To the extent that domestic adoptions have occurred, they often are done secretly, making it difficult to assess the extent to which incountry adoptions occur [Cox 1999]. Recognizing the barriers to domestic adoptions, the Korean Government in 1994 made the decision to allow continued international adoption of children who are not full Korean or who have disabilities [Reitman 1999].

Historically, U.S. citizens have adopted very few children from Africa. In 1998, only 96 children from Ethiopia, the African country from which the largest number of children come, were adopted [U.S. Department of State 1999]. International adoptions of African children outside of Ethiopia are extremely limited or nonexistent, as most African countries do not permit the adoption of children by citizens of other countries [Altstein & Simon 1991; Hester 1999]. It is not clear to what extent U.S. families would have an interest in adopting children from African nations if greater opportunities to adopt these children were made available.

The Policy Debate

There has been great debate regarding the international adoption of children, who generally come from less developed nations, by families who most often reside in developed countries. Three major positions on intercountry adoption have emerged. The first position opposes intercountry adoption; the second position views international adoption as uniformly positive for all concerned; and the third emphasizes that there are positive and negative aspects of intercountry adoption that affect both the individuals involved in these adoptions—birth families, adopted children, and adoptive parents—and the nations that are involved— children's birth countries and the so-called "receiving" countries [Westhues & Cohen 1994]. Each of these positions implicitly or explicitly addresses the issues of race, culture, and national origin as they affect children who are adopted internationally, their birth and adoptive families, their countries of origin, and their adoptive countries.

Opposition to intercountry adoption has equated it with colonialism, and, in some cases, cultural genocide [Ngabonziza 1988; Organization of American States 1984; Tolfree 1978]. Mrs. Schevardnadze, the First Lady of Georgia (Former Soviet Union), for example, has openly opposed the international adoption of Georgian children as an issue of national identity [Stanley 1997]. Others focus on inequities of power, with concerns that international adoption exploits the poor and women, creating situations in which birth parents may place their children for adoption without understanding the meaning of adoption or out of a sense of financial desperation [see Bagley 1993a, 1993b]. Still others base their opposition to international adoption on the negative impact of such adoptions on children's sense of racial and cultural identity [Barrett & Aubin 1990; McRoy 1991; Ryan 1983]. This issue is more fully explored later in this section.

Advocates of intercountry adoption, generally from the more developed countries in which prospective adoptive parents live, maintain that the practice meets the needs of homeless and abandoned children who otherwise would have lived in institutions until adulthood or who would have died from conditions in their birth countries [Bowen 1992; Joe 1978]. Bartholet [1996, p. 197], for example, writes:

> But there can be little doubt that overwhelming numbers
> of children in the poor countries of the world are living

and dying in conditions which involve extreme degrees of deprivation, neglect, exploitation, and abuse. These are the real problems of the children of the world. International adoption should be seen as an opportunity to solve some of these problems for some children.

Some advocates of international adoption are particularly critical of the position of those who oppose international adoption on grounds of national identity and responsibility. Bartholet [1996, pp. 207-208] writes:

> It seems clear that the debate over international adoption has little to do with genuine concerns over risks to children. Children are being sacrificed to notions of group pride and honor. ... Sending countries can talk of their homeless children as 'precious resources' but it is clear that the last thing these countries actually need is more children to care for.

Others dismiss the opposition to international adoption as mere political correctness with little regard for the interests of children [see Hayes 1995; Joe 1978]. Generally, considerations related to race and culture are not addressed by those who view international adoption as wholly positive because the interests of children in being rescued from the deprived conditions of their native countries are deemed paramount. When issues related to racial and cultural identity are recognized, they generally are minimized as no "different in nature than the problems many of these children would face in their own land" nor any different than "those all immigrants face" [Bartholet 1996, p. 205].

The third position incorporates the concerns of those who oppose international adoption and the benefits perceived by those who unequivocally support it. This position is based on the premise that, ideally, the interests of children are best served when children are reared in families and environments that mirror their racial and cultural identities [Westhues & Cohen 1994]. It also, however, recognizes that there are circumstances in which children will not have the opportunity to grow up in families in their birth countries—such as in China where girls may be abandoned as a result of the "one child" policy—or where children will encounter extreme prejudice and few opportunities for healthy development because of the child's own characteristics—such as children who are illegitimate, abandoned, or of mixed racial heritage in countries with strong cultural values that stigmatize children with these backgrounds [Westhues & Cohen 1994]. In particular, children's racial and cultural identities or their status as orphans may subject them to racism and discrimination in their own countries of origin [Cox 1999; Hester 1999]. International adoption, from this perspective, places value on both the child's racial and cultural identity and national heritage and the needs of each child for a permanent family. It generally views international adoption as an alternative to be considered and utilized only when families in children's own countries are not available and requires of international adoption that a child's racial and cultural identity continue to be honored [Freivalds 1999].

The role of international adoption itself and the weight to be accorded considerations related to race, culture, and national origin likewise are subject to different views in the context of international law. The different approaches to these issues are reflected in the way international law defines the hierarchy of options to be utilized when children cannot or will not be raised by their birth families in their birth countries. The United Nations Convention on the Rights of the Child (CRC) and the Hague Convention on Protection of Children and Cooperation in Respect of Intercountry Adoption (Hague Convention) illustrate the differing approaches. The CRC places great weight on a child's racial, cultural, and national identity and explicitly establishes a preference for incountry adoption and foster care in a child's country of origin, with intercountry adoption (and institutionalization, for other reasons) defined as a measure of last resort. The CRC, which recognizes the right of a child to a family in its Preamble, in Article 5 defines "family" quite broadly, including "members of the extended family or community as provided by local custom," suggesting support for a broad range of incountry options that promote the child's racial, cultural, and national identity.

By contrast, the Hague Convention explicitly references only the child's family of origin and intercountry adoption. In its Preamble, the Hague Convention provides that countries should "as a matter of priority" take "appropriate measures to enable the child to remain in the care of his or her family of origin" and states, next, that "intercountry adoption may offer the advantage of a permanent family to a child for whom a suitable family cannot be found in his or her State of origin." This language appears to suggest a preference for incountry adoption over intercountry adoption. It also appears to signal a preference for intercountry adoption over incountry foster care or other non-permanent alternatives in the country of origin, as these latter options are not mentioned in the Convention. If this interpretation is correct, the Hague Convention may place less weight on a child's direct connection with his racial, cultural, and national identity than does the CRC with its emphasis on a broader range of incountry resources that sustain the child's connection to his or her birth country.

The Hague Convention, however, with regard to the determination by the country of origin that a child may be adopted internationally, states that the country must "give due consideration to the child's upbringing and to his or her ethnic, religious and cultural background" and determine, based on reports relating to the child and prospective adoptive parents, "whether the envisaged placement is in the best interests of the child" (Article 16). These provisions place obligations on countries of origin to take the child's ethnic, religious, and cultural background into account in approving an adoptive placement, but there are no requirements that the "receiving" country, the adoptive parents, or the country of origin take any action postadoption regarding the child's birth heritage.

As these positions suggest, there is a wide divergence of perspectives on the role of race, culture, and national origin for children for whom international adoption is considered. Two major questions arise in this regard. First is the broad question of the extent to which children "belong" in some fundamental way to their racial, cultural, and national communities. Is it "right" or "wrong" to place children with families of different races and cultures in other countries? Absent a definitive position on this issue, should particular weight be given to the maintenance of a child's racial and cultural identity and connection to his or her national roots in the country of origin? How do children's racial, cultural, and national origin interests compare to other interests of children, specifically their needs for permanent, loving families? Assuming some level of acceptance of international adoption, the second question relates to the extent to which there are obligations to support a child's racial and cultural identity and connection to his or her country of origin when a child is adopted internationally. Do families, professionals, and the countries in which internationally adopted children live have obligations to support children's racial and cultural identity? What obligation exists to support children's connections with their birth countries?

Racial, Cultural, and National Identity Interests and Obligations

There are competing views of the "morality" of international adoption [Triseliotis 1991], that is, the "rightness" or "wrongness" of separating children from their racial, cultural, and national communities. From the perspective of those who oppose intercountry adoption in any form and at any level, the argument is made that deprivation of a child's cultural or national heritage poses an irreparable loss, if not an affirmative harm to a child. Balanon [1989, p. 250], a Filipino critic of intercountry adoption, for example, questions whether the basic needs of children can be met outside their culture of origin and poses the question, "What advantage does the Western society offer to deprived children not only during their formative years but for the rest of their lives? What happens to the colored foreign children in a predominately White society when they grow up?" Melone [1976], similarly, has raised questions about the extent to which a child can become part of a different culture, contending that the severing of a child's ties to his or her culture is equivalent to other violent separations of children from their families and environments. D.S. Kim [1978] has expressed concern about the impact of a racist environment on the adjustment of international adoptees and questioned whether positive adjustment is achieved at the cost of ethnic identity and heritage.

At the other end of the spectrum are those who embrace international adoption as wholly positive, and who, from that perspective, maintain that a child's racial, cultural, and national identity is not of overriding importance. Hayes [1993], for example, minimizes the impact of racial and cultural differences between parents and children and contends that adoptive parents' promotion of their children's racial and cultural identification is unnecessary for positive psychological adjustment. Bartholet [1996] appears to agree with this assessment, drawing from the research a conclusion that there is no evidence that the absence of a satisfactory ethnic and cultural identity presents psychological harm to the international adoptee.

From the perspective of those who acknowledge the positive and negative aspects of international adoption, a child's race, culture, and national origin are viewed as significant aspects of identity. Sustaining children whenever possible within their countries of origin—either with their birth families or with adoptive families in their own country—is viewed as the preferred alternative [Freivalds 1999]. From this perspective, there are significant benefits when children maintain their connections to their racial and cultural heritage within the family of origin or culture of origin and maintain their national identity by birth. Proponents of this perspective, however, recognize that for many children, as important as their race-, culture-, and national origin-based needs are, there are compelling reasons to pursue international adoption in order to promote children's safety, physical and emotional well-being, and interest in a permanent family. Advocates of this perspective—unlike those who promote international adoption as uniformly positive—place emphasis on ongoing obligations to internationally adopted children in relation to their racial and cultural identity and their connections to their native countries.

A number of issues arise in connection with the internationally adopted child's race, culture and national origin. Do these children have compelling race-, culture-, and national origin-based needs? To the extent that such needs exist, are there obligations on the part of adoptive families, adoption professionals, and "receiving" countries to meet those needs? The existing body of research on outcomes for children adopted internationally, specifically with regard to racial and cultural identity and children's experiences with racism and discrimination, provides some guidance on these issues. The practice literature likewise identifies and addresses some of the key issues that warrant consideration in relation to children's racial and cultural identities. This body of work principally addresses issues that affect children whose racial and cultural backgrounds differ from that of their adoptive families. By contrast, the literature has only minimally addressed issues that affect children who physically resemble their adoptive families but whose national origin, as opposed to racial or cultural origin, is the distinguishing factor. It should be noted that both the research and practice literature consider the issues of race, culture, and national origin in the context of adoption by Caucasian parents, reflecting the prevalent demographics of individuals who choose to adopt internationally.

Research on Outcomes

A significant body of research on the adjustment and adaptive functioning of children adopted internationally has been developed in the United States, England, Norway, Denmark, Sweden, Finland, Belgium, and Canada [Westhues & Cohen 1994]. This research, however, has produced varying results [Tizard 1991]. Some studies report that children who have been adopted from other countries are at greater risk of adjustment problems [Harder 1987; Kim et al. 1979; Kim, P.S. 1980; Rathburn et al. 1965; Saetersdal & Dalen 1991; Verhulst et al. 1990; Versluis-den Bieman & Verhulst 1995]. Other studies suggest that international adoptees are likely to encounter difficulties only in the initial period of adjustment following the adoptive placement [Cederblad 1982; Gunnarby et al. 1982]. Some studies suggest that adjustment problems are associated with older age at time of placement [Cederblad 1982; Gardell 1979; Hofvander et al. 1978], although other studies indicate that there is no such relationship [Bagley & Young 1980; Pruzan 1977]. One group of studies compares nonadopted children with children who are internationally adopted and finds no differences between the two groups of children [Bagley & Young 1980; Bagley 1991; Hoksbergen 1987; Kuhl 1985; Pruzan 1977]. In other studies, no control group is used, but findings suggest that internationally adopted children do, in general, function well [Gravel & Roberge 1984; Kim, D.S. 1978; Simon & Altstein 1977, 1981, 1987].

The differences in research findings on the adjustment and adaptive functioning of international adoptees may be attributed to a number of factors: a variety of research designs and tools; use of different data collection procedures; and differences in the populations of international adoptees studied in terms of age at placement, age at the time of the study, countries of origin, and the countries in which the children were living at the time of the study [Westhues & Cohen 1994]. With only a few exceptions [Gravel & Roberge 1984; Verhulst et al. 1990], the samples in the reported studies have been small and nonrepresentative [Westhues & Cohen 1994]. In addition, control groups have been limited to non-adopted children in the children's new home countries and have not provided a comparison between children who are internationally adopted and children who remain in orphanages or other institutional settings in their birth countries.

The research has explored the outcome measure most relevant to the focus of this book—a child's sense of racial and cultural identity—to only a limited extent [Westhues & Cohen 1994]. W.J. Kim [1995, p. 152] notes, "In comparison to the emphasis on 'blackness' of black children adopted by white families and white adoptive parents' familiarity with black culture, there has been little discussion of ethnic heritage of foreign-born children adopted by American families." Because racial and cultural identification and pride have been shown to play important roles in self-esteem and overall psychological adjustment of adolescents of color in general [Phinney 1991; Phinney & Alipuria 1990; Phinney & Rosenthal 1992], the extent to which international adoptees achieve a strong and positive sense of racial and cultural identity would appear to be a critical issue.

A few studies have explored the impact of international adoption on racial and cultural identity. In the U.S., the earlier studies focused on the initial and long-term adjustment of Korean adoptees [Chartrand 1979; D. S. Kim 1976], and later studies considered outcomes for broader groups of international adoptees, including children from Vietnam and Colombia [Harvey 1983; Linowitz & Boothby 1988; Melchoior 1986; Wilkinson 1981]. D.S. Kim's research [1977] in the mid-1970s focused on a range of outcomes for Korean children adopted by U.S. families. Findings indicated that adopted Korean children fared well in all aspects of their lives, including self-concept, socialization, and overall adjustment, an outcome the researcher associated with warm and supportive family environments. Kim did find, however, that adolescents who were adopted before their first birthday tended to have higher levels of self-esteem, adjustment, and personality integration than adolescents who had been adopted after their sixth birthday. On the issue of racial and cultural identity, Kim found that most Korean adoptees thought of themselves as "American." This finding led Kim [1978, p. 485] to comment that the critical role of racial and cultural identity for these children was being overlooked:

> It is necessary for the child to be aware of personal heritage to develop his full potential or to define his place in society. Therefore, while avoiding ethnocentricity or reverse racism, foreign children can and should be instilled with a positive ethnic identity. Such a positive identity formation can furnish children a useful inclination to self-assertion, advocacy, and determination for their full socialization.

Simon and Altstein, in the first wave of their study of Caucasian, African American, and Korean adoptees [1977], sought to learn whether children adopted transracially or transculturally had racial preferences, could indicate their own racial identity, and were aware of racial differences. Through the use of dolls and pictures, the researchers found that the children, then between the ages of four and seven, did not have a preference for white, brown, or black dolls or individuals shown in pictures. The researchers discovered that Caucasian and African American children were able in similar proportions to identify their own race, but they were not able to assess the ability of Korean children to do so because of the small number of Korean children participating and the construction of the test. They did find, however, that the three groups of children were similar in their level of racial awareness.

In the next wave of this study, Simon and Altstein [1992] found less clearly positive results with regard to racial and cultural identity than those suggested by their 1977 study. In this wave, they interviewed, in addition to adoptees from other racial groups, individuals adopted from Korea who were at that point in their twenties. They asked them, among other questions, what it meant to grow up in a family of a racial and cultural background that differed from their own. Sixty percent of the Korean adoptees stated that they did not remember when they first became aware of racial and cultural differences between themselves and their families, although among Korean adoptees who were adopted at age four or older, almost all said that they noticed the difference "immediately" or "at the time I was adopted." Although 45% stated that they "never" or "rarely" thought about being of a different race and culture than their adoptive families, most of the remaining 55% cited adolescence as the period in their lives when they found being of a different race and culture to be "harder." When asked how other Koreans reacted to them during their adolescence, 53% said that there were very few or no Koreans in their lives during that time period; 34% replied that the response was neither positive nor negative; and 26% reported that others "reacted negatively toward me." When asked "how do you think being Korean by birth but reared by white parents has affected the way you perceive yourself today?", one-third believed that it did not affect their self-image; one-third thought that it had a positive effect; one-fifth believed it had a negative impact; and 5% indicated that it had a highly negative effect. More than 60% of the Korean adoptees stated that Caucasian parents who have the opportunity to adopt a young Korean child should be sensitive to the child's birth culture.

Feigelman and Silverman [1983] similarly considered the adaptation of transracially and transculturally adopted individuals and found that, like African Americans adopted transracially, Asian and Latin American adoptees seemed to adapt reasonably well. Particularly in adolescence, international adoptees appeared to have better adjustment overall than either African Americans or Caucasians adopted domestically. With regard to the issue of racial and cultural identity, African American adoptees appeared to express greater pride in their racial heritage than did Koreans in their racial and cultural heritage. Seventy percent of the African American transracial adoptees stated that they "sometimes" or "often" proudly referred to being African American, whereas only 57% of the Korean transracial adoptees and 50% of the Colombian adoptees reported feelings of racial or cultural pride. The researchers, however, found that Korean adoptees who were better adjusted had more pride in their racial and cultural heritage. Their sense of cultural identity, however, diminished over time so that by adolescence, 63% of the Korean adoptees identified "primarily with white society" [1983, p. 156].

The Search Institute [Benson et al. 1994] also considered issues of racial and cultural identity for Korean adoptees, among other issues, in its study of families who adopted infants between 1974 and 1980. The responses of the 173 Korean adoptees [of the total of 881 adopted children who were subjects of the study] suggested a moderate level of comfort with their racial and cultural identity. Fifty-one percent of the Korean adoptees, for example, agreed with the statement, "Other people of my racial background accept me as one of them" and 54% agreed with the statement, "I get along better with people of my racial back-ground." Importantly, 22% of the Korean adoptees agreed with the statement that "I wish I was a different race than I am." Similarly, 21% disagreed with the statement "My parent(s) want me to be proud of my racial background," and 34% disagreed with the statement that "My parent(s) try hard to help me be proud of my racial background."

Andujo [1988] focused in her research on the cultural identity of adopted Mexican American adolescents and found that Mexican American children adopted by Caucasian families and by Mexican American families showed similar levels of self-esteem. Differences emerged, however, in the adoptees' views of themselves from a cultural perspective. None of the adolescents adopted by Caucasian families viewed themselves as Mexican American, whereas three-quarters of those adopted by Mexican American parents referred to themselves as Mexican American. Differences also were apparent in the parents' attitudes toward their children's birth cultures: 80% of the Caucasian parents emphasized their culture and de-emphasized Mexican American culture, whereas 87% of the Mexican American parents placed emphasis on Mexican American culture and reared their children in that cultural tradition.

In general, the research has yielded positive results on measures of self-esteem and psychological adjustment for international adoptees, but it also suggests that children who are adopted internationally are less likely to develop a strong racial or cultural identity than are children raised within their own racial and cultural communities [Andujo 1988; Bagley 1991; McRoy 1991; McRoy et al. 1982, 1984; McRoy & Zurcher 1983; Simon & Altstein 1987]. For some percentage, generally a small proportion of international adoptees, there may be significant identity confusion. Westhues and Cohen [1994], in their sample of internationally adopted adolescents in three Canadian provinces, for example, found that 10% of the adolescents—all of whom were from Korea, Bangladesh, and Haiti—considered themselves "white," identifying with the dominant racial culture. Similarly, Bagley

[1991] found that approximately 10% of Korean adoptees adopted by British families experienced confusion regarding their racial identity. Westhues and Cohen [1994, p. 152] observe that these adoptees' inaccurate perceptions of their "white" racial heritage may indicate that "there is a risk of [their] losing a sense of how they present themselves to the world." The misperception of racial identity may suggest a denial of racial identity, identity confusion, and potential difficulties coping with racism. Alternatively, Westhues and Cohen [1994] state that this self-perception, though inaccurate, could be positively interpreted as indicating that these adoptees' level of social acceptance is so great that they are not aware of their racial differences.

A second issue related to racial and cultural identity, which the research has explored to only a limited extent, is the experience of internationally adopted children and adolescents with racism. The research suggests that many internationally adopted adolescents of color experience unpleasant racial incidents as they get older [Triseliotis 1993], and some have expressed concern that the increased anti-immigration sentiment in the United States, as well as in other Western countries, may put internationally adopted children at greater risk of discrimination [Friedlander 1999]. The current body of research suggests that a significant number of international adoptees experience racism and discrimination, but that the impact of these experiences on their well-being and adjustment may be limited.

Kuhl [1985], in his study of international adoptees, found that half of the adolescents he interviewed had been belittled about their race. Simon and Altstein [1992] report that 65% of the parents they interviewed indicated that their children had reported at least one situation in which they were insulted because of their race. In the Danish study of Rorbech [1991], 27% of international adoptees reported being teased at school about their appearance. Bagley's Canadian study [1991] likewise found that international adoptees experienced racial insults in school (15%), higher than the Caucasian children in his study (none reported this experience) but much less than adopted Native children

(51.3%). In their study of Canadian adolescents who had been internationally adopted, Westhues and Cohen [1994, p. 13] found a substantially higher level of racial teasing than did Bagley: more than 80% of the adolescents they interviewed reported "a nasty or unpleasant experience because of their ethnic or racial background."

The research, however, seems to suggest that international adoptees experience a limited level of stress as a result of racial or cultural hostility, although a number of questions remain as to these findings. Several studies have suggested that racial hostility plays a minor role in the lives of Korean adoptees and their adoptive families [Keltie 1969; Kim, D.S. 1977]. Feigelman and Silverman [1983] similarly found that although Korean, Vietnamese, and Colombian adoptees and their adoptive families experienced some level of ethnic hostility, most families did not perceive this issue as harmful or ongoing. Other research [McRoy et al. 1982, 1984], however, indicates that the Caucasian families of international adoptees tend to minimize the effects of racial taunting, bringing into question the accuracy of family perceptions about the harmfulness to their children of ethnic hostility. In a similar vein, Versluis den-Bieman and Verhulst [1995] found that racism did not significantly impact the functioning of adolescents who had been adopted internationally by Dutch families, at least not to the extent that the adolescents' behavior would be considered deviant. Deviancy, however, may represent a relatively high standard for determining whether racism has an impact on the international adoptees whom they interviewed.

These research findings raise important questions: How do international adoptees as adolescents and as young adults—as opposed to the children and their adoptive families primarily interviewed in the research—view their experiences with racism and discrimination? Do these experiences affect their overall well-being, sense of belonging and sense of racial and cultural identity? Have these experiences changed over time? Would the findings of the research—much of which is from the late 1960s through 1980s—be duplicated if the research were conducted today?

Finally, do the experiences of international adoptees vary depending on the nature and level of diversity of the environments in which they are raised?

The Practice Literature

The literature on international adoption seems to suggest that race, culture, and national origin are important considerations for international adoptees and their families, but that these issues may have different implications depending on the extent to which children and their adoptive families physically resemble one another. The practice literature that addresses issues of race and culture for internationally adopted children has focused almost exclusively on families in which there are obvious racial and/or cultural differences between children and their parents—adoptions of Asian, indigenous Latin American or African children by Caucasians. Little has been written with regard to the cultural- or national origin-based needs of children who physically resemble the Caucasian parents who adopt them—children, for example, from Russia or Eastern Europe or from certain Latin American countries. The question arises as to whether different issues are posed by the two situations.

Race and Culture in Multiracial/Multicultural Families

Kirk's work on "acknowledgment of differences" in relation to adoptive and birth family formation [1984]—in which he correlates positive outcomes with the ability of adoptive families to acknowledge the differences between families formed through adoption and biological families—may have applicability in international adoption when children are physically different in very distinct ways from their adoptive parents [Trolley et al. 1995]. A child's racial characteristics or physical characteristics associated with a cultural or national heritage—when they differ from those of the adoptive parents—prompt, by necessity, an acknowledgment that the child is adopted [Trolley et al. 1995]. The extent to which the child's birth heritage, however, is clearly and unequivocally acknowledged may be more variable.

Some writers believe that acknowledgment of a child's racial, cultural, and national heritage should be as forthright as the acknowledgment of the adoption itself, and they express concerns that the heritage of internationally adopted children often is not appropriately recognized. Trolley and colleagues [1995, p. 467] observe that there may be an attempt on the part of many adoptive families to "Americanize" children "without a second thought to their birth culture." In other families, there may be active resistance to preserving the child's culture of origin. Trolley and colleagues [1995, p. 468], for example, note:

> The lack of acknowledgment of the birth culture may stem from adults' lack of understanding of the culture of origin, or their own bias toward American superiority as unconsciously perpetuated in the common euphemism "the adoption of foreign children."

D. S. Kim [1978] and Melone [1976] have expressed concerns about the psychological impact on adoptees when their racial and cultural heritage is treated as relatively insignificant or is ignored. They emphasize the critical role of racial and cultural identity in the self-worth of children of color and the effect on children's overall psychological adjustment and well-being when their families appear to discount these aspects of their identities. Some writers have focused on the particularly harmful effects of a failure to acknowledge the child's birth heritage when children are adopted at an older age. Kim and colleagues [1979], for example, describe the "shock of transplantation" for children adopted internationally at older ages, an experience that may precipitate identity crises as a result of the loss of birth parents and of their racial and cultural roots. The loss of the child's culture combined with the need to learn a new language and incorporate a new cultural environment have been viewed as a common developmental disability for these children [Hoksbergen 1991; Myer & James 1989].

On the other hand, there are those who believe that "Americanization" is necessary for children's survival and an overem-

phasis on a child's birth culture may subject children to discrimination [see Trolley et al. 1995]. Recognizing the potential harm of
overemphasizing the child's birth heritage, Friedlander [1999, p. 45]
asks, "Does having strong feelings or identification with his or her
culture of origin provide the child with a sense of security when faced
with prejudice and discrimination, or does ethnic identification
promote feelings of confusion, isolation, and alienation?"

The complexities of achieving and sustaining a positive racial
and cultural identity in an environment in which an individual is
clearly "different" are well recognized. There is consensus that at
very early ages, children of races other than their parents are aware
that they look different than their adoptive parents [McRoy 1991;
Mussen et al. 1969; Proshansky 1965]. This recognition of
differentness raises significant issues for children with regard to
attachment and belonging [Friedlander 1999]. Wilkinson [1995, p.
180], for example, writes:

> This awareness [of looking different] is intensified when
> [international adoptees] begin their school career. Other
> children notice and bring it up, sometimes out of curios-
> ity or prejudice and sometimes as a weapon. If the
> children are living in a geographical area with no other
> person of similar ethnicity, it is hard for them to accept
> their differences and feel alright [sic] about them, al-
> though they may become proficient at handling unpleas-
> ant situations.

International adoptees may face ongoing challenges through
adolescence and early adulthood in forging and sustaining an
identity that integrates their birth heritage. Racial and cultural
identity issues may have particular relevance to the task of
identity formation in adolescence, a process of determining "what
[adolescents] appear to be in the eyes of others as compared with
what they feel they are" [Erikson 1950, p. 261]. When internationally adopted young people do not racially resemble their adoptive
parents, the process may include, in addition to the usual developmental tasks associated with adolescence—friendships and
social relationships, future goals, sexual orientation and behavior,
and religious and moral values—tasks associated with integrating

their race and culture into their personal identity [Wilkinson 1995]. This process may be further complicated by what some clinicians have called "double-consciousness," the stressful experience in which an individual simultaneously identifies with two cultures but feels detached from both [Stonequist 1935]. In adolescence, for example, internationally adopted young people from Asia, Latin America, or Africa may find that Caucasians are not interested in a dating relationship with them, but that other adolescents of color ostracize them for "acting white" [Friedlander 1999]. As young adults, international adoptees may find that they are subjected to discrimination in the country in which they have been raised, are rejected by those who immigrate to the U.S. from their birth countries, and are considered "outsiders" when they visit their countries of birth.

Wilkinson [1981] hypothesizes that there are five stages of adaptation that may characterize the process by which internationally adopted individuals come to define and accept their racial and cultural identity:

- *Denial:* actively ignoring anything to do with the individual's racial or cultural group;

- *Inner awakening:* quietly beginning to take notice of others who are racially or culturally like the individual and of aspects of the race and/or culture to which the individual belongs;

- *Acknowledgment:* identifying and discussing racial and cultural differences in a positive way;

- *Identification:* actively connecting with others of the individual's race and culture to gain information and incorporate values—a phase that may prompt the rejection of the majority culture and idealization of the individual's racial or cultural group; and

- *Acceptance:* emergence of a balanced sense of pride in the individual's race and culture and an ability to comfortably function in the larger society—a phase when difficult memories associated with pre-adoption experiences may surface for individuals adopted at older ages.

This adaptational process may present significant challenges. The ability of international adoptees to develop a racial or cultural identity or understand the traditions of their countries of birth may be complicated by having no real recollection of their cultures because they were adopted as infants or very young children [Friedlander 1999]. In the absence of memories of the individual's birth country and any reference group that shares the individual's birth heritage, it may be difficult to forge a racial or cultural identity that integrates the individual's birth heritage.

The literature suggests that adoptive families play a significant role in supporting their children's positive racial and cultural identities. Rios-Kohn [1998, p. 4] highlights the responsibility of adoptive families to pay "due regard ... to the child's ethnic, religious, cultural and linguistic background." Westhues and Cohen [1994, p. 183] similarly emphasize the role of the adoptive family in "maintaining an identification with the ethno-racial origins of the children who are adopted crossnationally." The literature suggests that many adoptive parents take this responsibility quite seriously and in fact, make the decision to adopt internationally because of their interest in and appreciation of a particular culture [Bagley 1993b; Carstens & Julia 1995; Hoksbergen 1991]. Practitioners indicate, for example, that adoptive parents of Chinese children generally enter into adoption fully expecting that race and culture will be highly meaningful to their children and become very engaged with Chinese culture [Cox 1999]. The issue that is faced by many adoptive families, nonetheless, is the nature and scope of the activities in which they should engage in order to support their children's racial and cultural heritage. Freivalds [1999] notes that there is little guidance for adoptive parents as to what is and is not helpful for children, nor what level of involvement with their children's birth heritage is appropriate. She poses as examples of the types of issues which adoptive parents confront, "Is going to an ethnic restaurant enough? Should the family leave their church and join a Korean church instead? Are a few weeks of culture camp sufficient or should the family relocate to an ethnically diverse neighborhood?"

Although there are many questions related to the specific ways in which adoptive families may support their children's connections with their birth heritage, experts in international adoption appear to agree on the importance of the adoptive family's respect for and appreciation of diversity in general and their child's birth culture, in particular—irrespective of the child's current level of interest in her cultural heritage [Freivalds 1999; Hester 1999]. Huh [1997], for example, found in his research that when adoptive parents were actively involved in Korean culture, Korean adoptees had strong Korean identities and tended to identify themselves as Korean American rather than Korean, which he concluded was indicative of good identity integration. Huh found that in these supportive family environments, most Korean adoptees, by the time they reach 12 to 14 years of age, were able to integrate into their identities their Korean heritage and American culture.

The literature and research also suggest that adoptive families play a significant role in assisting their children to cope with racism and discrimination but that many adoptive families are uncertain as to how to provide their children with the necessary coping skills. In her research, Andujo [1988] found that Caucasian families tended to use an educational rather than experiential approach to assist their Mexican American adopted children in learning about their heritage and that they tended to minimize the importance of racial incidents. By contrast, Mexican American parents were more likely to live in Latino communities and to teach their children specific skills in responding to racism. Similarly, Feigelman and Silverman [1983] and McRoy and colleagues [1982, 1984] found that many Caucasian families, uncertain of how to help their children cope with racism, tended to minimize the importance of racial taunting. The research of Westhues and Cohen [1994] likewise suggested that many of the Caucasian parents of the Canadian international adoptees whom they studied underestimated the degree of discomfort that their children felt in the majority culture.

As families struggle with issues related to racism and discrimination, an important question arises regarding the weight that should be placed on a child's birth heritage and on the child's identification with the cultural traditions of the country in which he or she is being raised. Trolley and colleagues [1995, p. 468], in addressing this issue, distinguish between an individual's awareness of his or her birth culture and an identification with that culture to such an extent that the individual becomes "deviant from their peers." They emphasize the critical role of adoptive parents in preserving "the culture of origin on some level in order that these children can accept all aspects of themselves" [1995, p. 468], but they highlight that acknowledging both the adoption and the child's birth culture should be done in a normalizing manner [Trolley et al. 1995]. Other writers similarly emphasize that a balance is best achieved when the child's birth culture is integrated in daily life activities, and contacts and relationships are developed with others who share the child's heritage [Feigelman & Silverman 1983; Joe 1978]. As Westhues and Cohen note [1994, p. 183], when children cross racial and cultural lines in their family relationships:

> The challenge for policymakers, service providers, and most particularly the parents who adopt crossnationally will be to find that special balance that permits a child to acknowledge his or her roots while experiencing a sense of belonging and acceptance within their new family and culture.

National Origin

Different issues may be presented when internationally adopted children racially and culturally resemble their adoptive families. Research suggests that from a psychological perspective, racial and cultural identity is less critical to self-esteem for Caucasians than for people of color [Phinney 1991; Phinney & Alipuria 1990]. From a social perspective, internationally adopted children whose racial identity is Caucasian are more likely to identify and be identified with the dominant racial culture of the United States, irrespective of their national origin. As a consequence, it may be that international adoptees whose physical appearance is Caucasian—such as adoptees from Russia or Eastern Europe—may confront fewer identity-based issues in connection with their international adoption and experience less discriminatory behavior than internationally adopted children whose physical appearance is Asian, African, or reflective of indigenous peoples of Latin America [see Feigelman & Silverman 1983].

These psychological and social aspects of the experiences of international adoptees whose physical appearances mirror that of Caucasians born in the United States raise questions related to their personal identity in relation to national origin. When an adoptee physically resembles her adoptive family racially and culturally, are there equivalent identity issues associated with birth heritage? When a child "blends in" racially and culturally, are aspects of her national origin and culture of equivalent value to those of a child whose racial and cultural heritage is distinct from that of her adoptive family?

The literature has not addressed these issues to any meaningful extent. Experts in international adoption, however, suggest these children confront compelling issues related to their birth histories that impact their sense of personal identity and self-worth, irrespective of their physical resemblance in racial terms to their adoptive families. Freivalds [1999] highlights the importance of a child's understanding her origins, including the country where she was born and why she was "removed" from her birth country. A range of issues related to national origin may arise. A child adopted from Russia or Eastern Europe, for example, may have questions about the "acceptability" of her birth place, particularly from the perspective of her adoptive family, as well as concerns about why she was "rescued" from her country of origin while other children remained behind [Freivalds 1999]. Likewise, an internationally adopted child may have questions about what life would have been like for her if she had remained in her birth country. Although many children may view their international adoption as providing them with a quality of life unattainable in their countries of birth, other children may wonder whether life would have been better because they would have grown up in the culture in which they were born [Freivalds 1999].

Experts in international adoption highlight the reality that children who are adopted internationally have very little information about their birth parents, and consequently, information about the "mother country" can play a significant role in providing the child with a sense of history and identity [Hester 1999]. From such information, the child can construct a history for herself—an aspect of her identity that is as important for a child who physically resembles her adoptive parents as for a child whose racial and cultural background is obviously different. Hester [1999] and Cox [1999] also point out that a child's understanding of her national origin may include the need to come to terms with the economic realities faced by her birth family and her country of origin in general. Hester [1999] notes that it may be easy for a child and her adoptive family to connect with the predominant culture of a country as expressed in the arts, literature, or food, but that a recognition of the prevailing poverty in countries from which internationally adopted children come is equally powerful in helping a child understand the circumstances involved in her adoption. This understanding, however, may also precipitate concerns on the child's part, including a sense of "survivor's guilt" and worry about the well-being of the birth family and any siblings she may have [Freivalds 1999].

A final consideration related to an international adoptee's national origin-based needs is the interest of some adoptive parents in adopting only children whose physical characteristics mirror the family's racial and cultural features, a choice designed to avoid issues related to birth heritage. Experts in international adoption acknowledge that there are parents who seek to adopt from Russia or Eastern Europe in order to have a "Caucasian child without a birth parent" and to obviate the need to acknowledge the cultural or national heritage of their adopted child [Freivalds 1999; Hester 1999]. From the perspective of these experts, this view of international adoption as a "simpler" way to adopt is fraught with difficulties for the child and the adoptive family. International adoption, according to these experts, presents greater challenges because of the inherent limitations on the background information that is available for many children adopted internationally—a situation that may have profound consequences for a child's psychological, social, and physical well being [Freivalds 1999; Hester 1999]. When, in addition to the realities of limited personal information on the child, adoptive families make the deliberate choice to avoid validation of their child's birth parents or any recognition of their child's cultural and national heritage, the child is likely to be left with no connections to her origins. In the words of one expert, this approach to international adoption represents a "real loss" for the child and the family [Hester 1999].

Other Considerations

Three additional considerations bearing on race, culture, and national origin should be noted. In each of these areas—search and reunion in the international context, the "culture" of institutions, and the adoption of U.S. children by families in other countries— there is little research and only a limited practice base of knowledge. Experts in the field of international adoption, however, point to important issues in each of these areas that warrant close attention.

Search and Reunion

Although interest is increasing among international adoptees regarding search and reunion and there is a growing number of successful searches [Cox 1999], it is not clear how many adoptees have contact with their birth parents or extended families in their countries of origin [Friedlander 1999]. Search and reunion have been pursued more commonly by Korean adoptees, who as a group, are of an age to express an interest in and attempt to search. Many other international adoptees—particularly from China, Russia, and the Republics of Eastern Europe where international adoption is a more recent phenomenon—are as yet too young to be involved with search at any level.

The literature does not address search in the international context to any significant degree. Experts such as Cox [1999], however, indicate that search may have different meanings for international adoptees than for domestic adoptees. For many individuals who were adopted internationally, search is limited to an exploration of the adoptee's racial and cultural heritage and a desire to experience the country of his or her birth. For these adoptees, the interest is in the culture and history of the country from which they came rather than a desire to find their birth families. Other adoptees may wish to search for and meet their birth parents, a possibility that is, in general, more remote for international adoptees than for individuals adopted in the United States. In the context of searching for birth parents, Cox [1999] points out that cultural values and traditions pose significant issues. An understanding of the impact of these cultural consider-ations has developed most fully in relation to Korea—the country in which the majority of international search efforts occur because of the longer history of intercountry adoptions.

Broad differences between Western thought, values, atti-tudes, and communication patterns and those that characterize Korean culture affect efforts to search as well as the nature of the contact with birth families when it is made [Cox 1999]. Because adoptees are not likely to understand the cultural gulf between themselves and their birth families, Cox [1999] emphasizes the need for Korean adoptees to first "search" for their Korean heritage and develop an understanding of those cultural traditions before seeking their birth families. This level of search concentrates on cultural traditions and nuances, including communication styles that may be radically different from Western communication patterns [Cox 1999]. In addition to the broad cultural differences between Korea and the U.S., the cultural values and traditions of Korea may also affect the extent to which an adoptee's efforts to search for his or her birth parents will be accepted. On the one hand, cultural values may make search and reunion more difficult, particularly when the adoption was planned by the birth mother because she was unmarried. In these cases, there may be very limited information available and a reluctance to share existing information with a searching adoptee because of cultural values that continue to stigmatize unmarried mothers [Freivalds 1999]. On the other hand, cultural values may promote the sharing of information to facilitate a search and reunion. Many adoptions of Korean children have taken place because of the extreme financial hardship suffered by their birth families [Cox 1999]. In these cases, considerable background information is often available and almost universally, there is a desire to reconnect adoptees and their birth families, based on the Confucian ethic that an individual is forever bound to his family by birth and although adopted is "always Korean first" [Cox 1999].

It is unclear to what extent search and reunion will be a part of the life experiences of adoptees from countries other than Korea, such as Russia, the countries of Eastern Europe, and Latin America. The fact that many of the children from Russia and Eastern Europe are placed for adoption as a result of parental alcoholism and extreme neglect sets a very different context for search and reunion than is the case for children adopted from Korea or other Asian countries [Cox 1999]. Other important differences between Asian and Eastern European countries may affect the nature and scope of any efforts on the part of adoptees to search for and be reunited with their birth families. There is, for example, no viable infrastructure within Russia and Eastern European countries that supports the gathering and retention of background information on children placed internationally for adoption, and these countries do not have the strong spiritual context that elevates the value of a child's connection with birth family, as is the case in Korea [Cox 1999]. With regard to Latin American countries, the concept of search and reunion may be so unfamiliar that the response of bureaucratic authorities will be bewilderment or even hostility [Hester 1999]. Cultural attitudes within the adoptee's birth country that view U.S. citizenship and adoption by Caucasian parents as indicative of higher status may render the adoptee's desire to search incomprehensible to local authorities [Hester 1999]. At the same time, the attitudes of adoptive parents in the U.S. may also play a role in the extent to which search and reunion may be pursued, particularly in cases in which adoptive parents have not placed emphasis on their children's cultural or national origins.

The "Culture" of Institutions

Most children adopted from Russia and Eastern Europe are adopted at young ages and, as a consequence, do not bring with them a sense of cultural identity in relation to their families and countries of birth. These children, by virtue of their physical appearance, are likewise not specifically identified with a particular culture or country of origin. They may, however, carry with them a sense of organizational "culture"—the culture of the orphanages or institutions in which they have been raised.

Experts in international adoption point out that this "cultural" background may, in fact, be the common variable in international adoption, irrespective of the country from which a child may come [Hester 1999]. Children enter these institutional settings early in life and the "culture" which they come to know is one often characterized by a level of care that is, at best, at a maintenance level and which, in some cases, involves abuse and exploitation [Hester 1999]. Pediatric and child psychiatry research suggest that infants and young children in orphanage care are at particular biologic and social risk in relation to physical health, particularly due to infectious disease; nutrition and growth; cognitive development; socioemotional development; and maltreatment [Frank et al. 1996]. Institutional placement also carries with it the stigma associated with being an orphan, an undesirable status in many countries and one which causes children to be treated as social outcasts [Cox 1999].

Because of these factors, the culture that children bring with them when they are adopted internationally may not be the larger culture of their countries—which as very young children they have not experienced—but the more narrow culture of institutions—with deleterious effects on children's physical, emotional, and developmental status. Hester [1999] notes that this reality may make concerns about children being taken "out of their culture" through international adoption largely theoretical. The more compelling issue may be the negative impact of the culture of the orphanage on the child's longer term health and well-being.

Intercountry Adoption of American Children

An aspect of international adoption that has received little attention is the adoption of children from the United States by families in other countries. Little is known about U.S. children who are adopted internationally and the families who adopt them, and consequently, little is understood about the extent to which these children, like children internationally adopted by U.S. families, encounter identity issues and discrimination based on their race, culture, and national origin. Some have surmised that the majority of children who leave the U.S. for international adoption are older children, minority children, and children with special physical, mental health, and developmental needs [Smolowe 1994]. Others have speculated that it is infants who are primarily placed with adoptive families in other countries, a practice attributed by some to the higher fees that families in Europe and Canada may be willing to pay in connection with the adoption of an infant [Smolowe 1994]. In the absence of any statistical data or a research or practice base of knowledge regarding internationally adopted U.S. children, it is difficult to address with any certainty questions related to the needs of U.S. children based on their racial and cultural heritage. It may be reasonable, however, to assume that their needs will be, in many ways, similar to the identity needs of children adopted from other countries by U.S. families.

When implementing legislation is enacted in connection with ratification of the Hague Convention on Intercountry Adoption, the U.S. will be required to monitor intercountry adoptive placements of U.S. children, as other countries currently do, and more information will be available regarding the characteristics of children who leave the U.S. for adoption. Ratification of the Hague

Convention, however, will bring into question issues related to U.S. policy on the role of race and culture in adoption. The approach to race and culture as stated in the Hague Convention ostensibly conflicts with U.S. policy on the role of race and culture in adoption as stated in MEPA. The Hague Convention requires that "states of origin," such as the U.S. when U.S. children are adopted by families in other countries, "give due consideration to the child's upbringing and to his or her ethnic, religious, and cultural background," a consideration that is to inform the country's assessment as to "whether the envisaged placement is in the best interests of the child" (Article 16). By contrast, MEPA prohibits the consideration of race, color or national origin in making an adoptive placement for a child with a family in the U.S.

These legal differences raise important questions. Are racial and cultural considerations more compelling when U.S. children are adopted internationally than when they are adopted domestically? Does an international adoption of an African American child by a Caucasian family in Canada, for example, require attention to the child's racial and cultural heritage whereas adoption of the same child by a Caucasian family in the U.S. does not? Should a Latino child's culture be disregarded if the prospective adoptive parents live in Vermont but given "due consideration" if the prospective adoptive family lives in England? The very different policy approaches demonstrated by U.S. law as embodied by MEPA, on the one hand, and the Hague Convention, to which the U.S. is a signatory, on the other, may reflect the uncertainty which permeates attitudes about and definitions of the appropriate role of race and culture in adoption in this country.

Summary

A number of critical issues arise in relation to the role of race, culture, and national origin in international adoption. What specifically should be the role of international adoption in relation to efforts within countries to support birth families and develop other incountry options? This ongoing issue recently resurfaced as international adoption was suggested as an alternative for children displaced as a result of the Kosovo conflict [Otto 1999]. International relief workers reported being "swamped" by "a flood of well-intentioned American offers of adoption" for children who had been separated from their families as they fled Kosovo [Otto 1999]. Apart from the fact that the focus of efforts for these children was to reunite them with their birth families rather than place them for adoption internationally, there clearly were issues related to race and culture in connection with the extraordinary level of interest in adopting these Caucasian children [Haven 1999], interest which did not surface when thousands of Somalian and Tibetan children were displaced as a result of civil war in those countries.

The research and literature suggest that race and culture play significant roles in identity for adoptees whose racial and cultural heritage differs from that of their adoptive parents. Are there obligations on the part of adoptive parents to support the development of their children's racial and culture identity and to provide their children with the necessary skills to cope with racism and discrimination? What is the obligation of adoption agencies in preparing, educating, and supporting adoptive parents to play these roles for their children? With regard to children whose physical appearance permits a "blending in" with mainstream American culture, including adoptees from Russian and Eastern Europe, is there an obligation to support these children's connections with their countries of origins? Should agencies support adoptive families who pursue international adoption with a primary goal of adopting a "Caucasian child without a birth family"?

Finally, how should the other many considerations related to race, culture, and national origin in international adoption be approached? How should search and reunion be viewed in the international context in light of significant cultural differences between the U.S. and countries of origin? To what extent does the "culture" of institutions represent the "real" culture that young children leave behind? And finally, what obligations exist regarding U.S. children's needs based on race, culture, and national origin when they are adopted by families in other countries?

Conclusion

The issues bearing on the role of race, culture, and national origin in adoption are multifaceted and complex. The field of adoption faces considerable challenges as it confronts issues related to the appropriate role of race and culture in the adoptive placements of children in foster care in this country; the role of culture in foster care for and the adoption of American Indian children; and the role of race, culture, and national origin in the international adoption of children by families in this country and the adoption of U.S. children by families in other countries. These issues have triggered considerable debate at both the practice and policy level, fueled not only by competing interests within adoption itself but by forces in the broader social and political environment.

This book has attempted to identify the critical issues bearing on race, culture, and national origin in adoption; synthesize the current knowledge base so as to strengthen the field's understanding of these issues; and analyze the various practice and policy perspectives that characterize the debates in this area. It is hoped that this review and analysis will provide a solid base on which an informed discussion of these critical issues may continue. It is only through such discussion that consensus can be reached on the appropriate role of race, culture, and national origin in adoption—and the ethical obligations of adoption professionals, public and private child welfare agencies, state, local, and tribal authorities, and society as a whole to the racially and culturally diverse children and families served through adoption.

References

Alba, R. (1990). *Ethnicity in America: The transformation of White America.* New Haven, CT: Yale University Press.

Alexander, R. Jr. & Curtis, C. M. (1996). A review of empirical research involving the transracial adoption of African American children. *Journal of Black Psychology, 22,* 223–235.

Almaguer, T. (1994). *Racial fault lines: The historical origins of white supremacy in California.* Berkeley: University of California Press.

Altstein, H. & Simon, R. J. (1991). Introduction. In H. Altstein & R. J. Simon (Eds.), *Intercountry adoption: A multinational perspective* (pp. 1–13). New York: Praeger.

Andujo, E. (1988). Ethnic identity of transethnically adopted Hispanic adolescents. *Social Work, 37,* 531–35.

Associated Press. (1997, October 14). Family protests whites' adoption of biracial twins. *Miami Herald.* [Online]. Available: http://www.herald.com:80/florida/digdocs/052988.htm.

Austin, D. (1988). *The political economy of human service programs.* Greenwich, CT: JAI Press.

Avery, R. J. (1998). Adoption assistance under PL 96-272: A policy analysis. *Children and Youth Services Review, 20*(1–2), 29–56.

Avery, R. J. & Mont, D. M. (1994). *Special needs adoption in New York State: Final report on adoptive parent survey.* [DHHS Contract No. 90CW1012]. Washington, DC: U.S. Department of Health and Human Services.

Bachrach, C. A., London, K. A., & Maza, P. L. (1991). On the path to adoption: Adoption seeking in the United States, 1988. *Journal of Marriage and the Family, 53,* 705–718.

Bachrach, C. A., Stolley, K. S., & London, K. A. (1992). Relinquishment of premarital births: Evidence from National Survey Data. *Family Planning Perspectives, 24*(2), 27–32, 48.

Bagley, C. & Young, L. (1980). The long-term adjustment and identity of a sample of inter-country adopted children. *International Social Work, 23*(3), 16–22.

Bagley, C. (1991). Adoption of Native children in Canada: A policy analysis and research report. In H. Altstein & R. J. Simon (Eds.),

127

Intercountry adoption: A multinational perspective (pp. 55–79). New York: Praeger.

Bagley, C. (1993a). Chinese adoptees in Britain: A twenty-year follow-up of adjustment and social identity. *International Social Work, 36,* 143–157.

Bagley, C. (1993b). Transracial adoption in Britain: A follow-up study, with policy considerations. *Child Welfare, 72,* 285–299.

Bakeis, C. D. (1996). The Indian Child Welfare Act of 1978: Violating personal rights for the sake of the tribe. *Notre Dame Journal of Law, Ethics and Public Policy, 10,* 543–586.

Balanon, L. G. (1989). Foreign adoption in the Philippines. *Child Welfare, 68,* 245–254.

Banks, R. R. (1998). The color of desire: Fulfilling adoptive parents' racial preferences through discriminatory state action. *Yale Law Journal, 107,* 875–964.

Barrett, S. E. & Aubin, C. M. (1990). Feminist considerations of intercountry adoption. *Women and Therapy, 10*(1–2), 127–138.

Barth, R. P. (1997). Effects of age and race on the odds of adoption versus remaining in long-term out-of-home care. *Child Welfare, 76,* 285–308.

Barth R. P., Courtney, M. E., Berrick, J. D., & Albert, V. (1994). *From child abuse to permanency planning: Child welfare services, pathways and placements.* New York: Aldine de Gruyter.

Barth R. P. & Berry, M. (1988). *Adoption and disruption.* New York: Aldine de Gruyter.

Bartholet, E. (1991). Where do Black children belong? The politics of race matching in adoption. *University of Pennsylvania Law Review, 139,* 1163–1256.

Bartholet, E. (1993). *Family bonds: Adoption and the politics of parenting.* New York: Houghton Mifflin Company.

Bartholet, E. (1996). International adoption: Propriety, prospects and pragmatics. *International Adoption, 13,* 181–210.

Bartholet, E. (1998). Testimony before the Subcommittee on Human Resources of the House Committee on Ways and Means. Hearing on Interethnic Adoptions. September 15. [On-line]. Available: www.house.gov/ways_means/humres/testmony/9-15-98/9-15bart.htm

Bausch, R. S. & Serpe, R. T. (1999). Recruiting Mexican American adoptive families. *Child Welfare, 78*, 693–716.

Bennett, M. K. (1993). Native American children: Caught in the web of the Indian Child Welfare Act. *Hamline Law Review, 16*, 953–973.

Benson, P. L., Sharma, A., & Roehlkepartain, E. C. (1994). *Growing up adopted: A portrait of adolescents and their families.* Minneapolis: Search Institute.

Bernal, M., Knight, G., Garza, C., Ocampo, K., & Cota, M. (1990). The development of ethnic identity in Mexican American children. *Hispanic Journal of Behavioral Sciences, 12*, 3–24.

Berrick, J. D., Barth, R. P., & Needell, B. (1994). A comparison of kinship foster homes and family foster homes: Implications for kinship as family preservation. *Children and Youth Services, 16*, 7–13.

Billingsley, A. (1992). *Climbing Jacob's ladder: The enduring legacy of African-American families.* New York: Simon & Schuster.

Billingsley, A. & Giovannoni, J. M. (1972). *Children of the storm: Black children and American child welfare.* New York: Harcourt, Brace, Jovanovich, Inc.

Blanchard, B. L. & Barsh, R. L. (1980). What is best for tribal children? A response to Fischler. *Social Work, 25*, 350–357.

Blauner, R. (1972). *Racial oppression in America.* New York: Harper & Row.

Bowen, J. (1992). *A Canadian guide to international adoptions: How to find, adopt, and bring home your child.* Vancouver, BC: Self-Counsel Press.

Bower, J.W. (1998). *Self-awareness tool: Are you ready to parent a child of another race, culture or ethnicity?* St. Paul, MN: North American Council on Adoptable Children.

Boyd-Franklin, N. (1989). *Black families in therapy: A multisystems approach.* New York: Guilford Press.

Bridget R. v. Cindy R. (1996). 41 Cal. App. 4th 1483, 49 Cal. Rptr. 507.

Brooks, C.M. (1994). The Indian Child Welfare Act in Nebraska: Fifteen years later, a foundation for the future. *Creighton Law Review, 27*, 661–708.

Brooks, D. & Barth, R. P. (1999). Adult transracial and inracial adoptees: Effects of race, gender, adoptive family structure, and placement history on adjustment outcomes. *American Journal of Orthopsychiatry, 69,* 87–99.

Brooks, D., Barth, R. P., Bussiere, A., & Patterson, G. (1999). Adoption and race: Implementing the Multiethnic Placement Act and the Interethnic Adoption Provisions. *Social Work, 44,* 167–175.

Brooks, D., Bussiere, A., Barth, R., & Patterson, G. (1997). *Adoption and race: Implementing the Multiethnic Placement Act of 1994 and the Interethnic Adoption Provisions.* Adoption and Race Work Group, convened by the Stuart Foundation. San Francisco: The Stuart Foundation.

Brown, A. W. & Bailey-Etta, B. (1997). An out-of-home care system in crisis: Implications for African-American children in the child welfare system. *Child Welfare, 76,* 65–83.

Byler, W. (1977). *The destruction of the American Indian families.* New York: Association on American Indian Affairs.

California Family Code. (1994). Section 8708.

Carleton, J. N. (1997). The Indian Child Welfare Act: A study in the codification of the ethnic best interests of the child. *Marquette Law Review, 81,* 21–45.

Carriere, J. L. (1994). Representing the Native American: Culture, jurisdiction, and the Indian Child Welfare Act. *Iowa Law Review, 79,* 585–652.

Carro, J. L. (1995). Regulation of intercountry adoption: Can the abuses come to an end? *American Journal of Family Law, 9,* 135–153.

Carstens, C. & Julia, M. (1995). Legal, policy and practice issues for intercountry adoptions in the United States. *Adoption and Fostering, 19*(4), 26–33.

Cederblad, M. (1982). *Children adopted from abroad and coming to Sweden after age three.* Stockholm: The Swedish National Board for Intercountry Adoptions.

Center for Early Education and Development. (1991). Why is attachment relationship important? *Fact Find* (p. 2). Minneapolis: University of Minnesota.

Chandra, A., Abma, J., Maza, P., & Bachrach, C. (1999). Adoption, adoption seeking, and relinquishment for adoption in the United States. *Advance Data,* 306. Washington, DC: Centers for Disease Control and Prevention/National Center for Health Statistics.

Chapin Hall Center for Children at the University of Chicago. (1997). *An update from the multistate foster care data archive: Foster care dynamics 1983-1994.* Chicago: Author.

Chartrand, W. (1979). Application of selected components of a correspondence theory of cross-cultural adjustment to the adjustment of white families who have adopted older children from Korea. *Dissertation Abstracts International, 39,* 9A.

Chestang, L. (1972). The dilemma of transracial adoption. *Social Work, 17,* 100–15.

Chestang, L. (1983). The policies and politics of health and human services: A Black perspective. In A.E. Johnson (Ed.), *The Black experience: Considerations for health and human services* (pp. 13–25). Davis, CA: International Dealogue Press.

Chestang, L.W. (1984). Racial and personal identity in the black experience. In B. W. White (Ed.), *Color in a white society* (pp. 83–95). Washington, DC: NASW Press.

Child Welfare League of America. (1992). Kinship care. A new look at an old idea. *Children's Voice, 1*(3), 6–7, 22.

Child Welfare League of America. (1995). *Child abuse and neglect: A look at the states.* Washington, DC: CWLA Press.

Child Welfare League of America. (1997). *Child abuse and neglect: A look at the states.* Washington, DC: CWLA Press.

Child Welfare Watch. (1998). Child removals: Dislocating the black family. *Child Welfare Watch, 3,* 4–7.

Chimezie, A. (1975). Transracial adoption of black children. *Social Work, 20,* 296–301.

Chipungu, S.S. (1991) A value-based policy framework. In J. E. Everett, S. S. Chipungu, & B. R. Leashore (Eds.), *Child welfare: An Africentric perspective* (pp.290–305). New Brunswick, NJ: Rutgers University Press.

Close, M. (1983). Child welfare and people of color: Denial of equal access. *Social Work, 28,* 13–20.

Cole, E. S. & Donley, K. S. (1990). History, values, and placement: Policy issues in adoption. In D. K. Brodzinsky and M. D. Schechter, (Eds.), *The psychology of adoption* (pp. 273–294). New York: Oxford University Press.

Coleman, N. (1996, December 29). Missing Denisha. *St. Paul Pioneer Press*, p. 1C.

Colorado Children's Code. (1993). Section 19-5-104.

Comer, J. P. & Poussaint, A. F. (1975). *Black child care: How to bring up a healthy Black child in America*. New York: Simon & Schuster.

Committee for Hispanic Children and Families. (1996). *Cultural competence and Latino adoption*. New York: Author.

Courtney, M. E. (1997). The politics and realities of transracial adoption. *Child Welfare, 76*, 749–780.

Courtney, M. E. & Needell, B. (1997). Outcomes of kinship foster care: Lessons from California. In J. D. Berrick, R. P. Barth, & N. Gilbert (Eds.), *Child Welfare Research Review* (Vol. II, pp. 130–149). New York: Columbia University Press.

Courtney, M. E., Barth, R. P., Berrick, J. D., Brooks, D., Needell, B., & Park, L. (1996). Race and child welfare services: Past research and future directions. *Child Welfare, 75*, 99–137.

Cox, C. B. & Ephross, P. H. (1998). *Ethnicity and social work practice*. New York: Oxford University Press.

Cox, S. (1999, May 3). Personal communication. Director of Public Policy and External Affairs. Holt International Children's Services, Eugene, OR.

Cross, T. (1986). Drawing on cultural traditions in Indian child welfare practice. *Social Casework, 67*, 283–289.

Cross, T. (1995). Establishing status of Indian children: Hearings on S. 1448 before the House Subcommittee on Native American and Insular Affairs, 104th Congress.

Crumbley, J. (1998). Training on transracial adoption: Impact of transracial adoption on the adopted child and the adoptive family (Tape A); Parental tasks, goals, and challengees in transracial adoptions (Tape C). Philadelphia: Author.

Cummings, C. (1998). Adopting from Russia: A war of perceptions. *Russian Life, 41*(6), 10–17.

Davis, T. H. (1993). The existing Indian family exception to the Indian Child Welfare Act. *North Dakota Law Review, 69*, 469–70.

Day, D. (1979). *Adoption of Black children*. Lexington, MA: Lexington Books.

DeBerry, K. M., Scarr, S., & Weinberg, R. (1996). Family racial socialization and ecological competence: Longitudinal assessments of

African-American transracial adoptees. *Child Development, 67,* 2375–2399.

Drummond v. Fulton. (1978). 563 F.2d 1200 (5th Cir. 1977) (en banc), *cert. denied*, 437 U.S. 910.

Dubowitz, H., Feigelman, S., & Zuravin, S. (1993). A profile of kinship care. *Child Welfare, 72,* 153–169.

Duncan, S. (1993, July 15). *Statement on transracial adoption.* Presented to the Senate Committee on Children, Family, Drugs and Alcoholism. On file at The Evan B. Donaldson Adoption Institute.

Dusky, L. (1996). *Still unequal: The shameful truth about women and justice in America.* New York: Crown Publishers.

Edmund S. Muskie Institute of Public Affairs. (1995) *Kinship care in America: A national policy study.* Portland: University of Southern Maine.

Edwards, D. (1999, June 14). Personal communication. Dr. Diana Edwards, Professor of Anthropology, Silver City, New Mexico.

English, D. & Clark, T. (1996). *Report of children in foster and group care placements in Washington State between June 1985 and August 1995.* Seattle, WA: Washington State Division of Children and Family Services, Office of Children's Administration Research.

Erikson, E. (1950). *Childhood and society.* New York: W.W. Norton.

Erikson, E. (1968). Race and the wider identity. In E. Erikson (Ed.), *Identity, youth and crisis* (pp. 295–320). New York: W.W. Norton.

Espiritu, Y. L. (1992). *Asian-American panethnicity.* Philadelphia: Temple University Press.

Everett, J. E., Chipungu, S. S., & Leashore, B. R. (Eds.). (1991). *Child welfare: An Africentric perspective.* New Brunswick, NJ: Rutgers University Press.

Family Impact Seminar. (1998). *Finding families for waiting kids: The challenge of special needs adoption in the 90's and beyond.* Washington, DC: Family Impact Seminar.

Fanshel, D. (1972). *Far from the reservation: The transracial adoption of American Indian children.* Metuchen, NJ: The Scarecrow Press.

Feigelman, W. (1998). *Adjustments of transracially and inracially adopted young adults.* Manuscript in preparation, on file with the Evan B. Donaldson Adoption Institute.

Feigelman, W. & Silverman, A. R. (1983). *Chosen children: New patterns of adoptive relationships.* New York: Praeger.

Feigelman, W. & Silverman, A. R. (1984). The long-term effects of transracial adoption. *Social Service Review, 8,* 588–602.

Feigelman, W. & Silverman, A. R. (1986). Adoptive parents, adoptees, and the sealed record controversy. *Social Casework, 67*(4), 219–226.

Fischler, R. S. (1980). Protecting American Indian children. *Social Work, 25,* 341–349.

Forte, L. (1997, August 24). Adoption adapts to race: Awareness up as cultures mix. *Chicago Sun-Times,* p. 21.

Foster, S. (1997, September 7). How race plays in the adoption game: Adoptions often based on parents' race. *The Salt Lake Tribune,* p. A1.

Frank, D. A., Klass, P. E., Earls, F., & Eisenberg, L. (1996). Infants and young children in orphanages: One view from pediatrics and child psychiatry. *Pediatrics, 97,* 569–578.

Frankel, M. (1995, June 16). Too good to be true. *Newsweek,* 18–20.

Frankenberg, R. (1993). *White women, race matters: The social construction of whiteness.* Minneapolis: University of Minnesota Press.

Freivalds, S. (1999, April 14). Personal communication with Coordinator of Hague Policy, Joint Council on International Children's Services, Washington, DC.

Friedlander, M. L. (1999). Ethnic identity development of internationally adopted children and adolescents: Implications for family therapists. *Journal of Marital and Family Therapy, 25*(1), 43–60.

Gallagher, B. D. (1994). Indian Child Welfare Act of 1978: The Congressional foray into the adoption process. *Northern Illinois University Law Review, 15,* 81–106.

Gardell, I. (1979). *A Swedish study on intercountry adoptions.* Stockholm: The Swedish Council for Intercountry Adoptions at the National Board of Health and Welfare.

Gershenson, C. (1984). *Community response to children freed for adoption.* Child Welfare Research Notes 3. Washington, DC: U.S. Department of Health and Human Services.

Gill, O. & Jackson, B. (1983). *Adoption and race.* London: St. Martin's Press.

Gill, B. (In press). Adoption agencies and the search for the ideal family, 1918–1965. In E. Wayne Carp, (Ed.), *Adoption in history: New interpretive essays.* Ann Arbor: University of Michigan Press.

Gilles, T. & Kroll, J. (1991). *Barriers to same-race placement.* St. Paul, MN: North American Council on Adoptable Children.

Gleeson, J. P. & Craig, L. C. (1994). Kinship care in child welfare: An analysis of state policies. *Children and Youth Services Review, 16* (1–2), 7–32.

Goddard, L. I. (1996). Transracial adoption: Unanswered theoretical and conceptual issues. *Journal of Black Psychology, 22*, 236–239.

Goerge, R. M. (1990). The reunification process in substitute care. *Social Service Review, 64*(3), 422–457.

Goerge, R. M., Wulczyn, F. H., & Harden, A. W. (1994). *Foster care dynamics: California, Illinois, Michigan, New York, and Texas—A first-year report from the Multistate Foster Care Data Archive.* Chicago: Chapin Hall Center for Children, University of Chicago.

Goerge, R. M., Wulczyn, F. H., & Harden, A. W. (1995). *Foster care dynamics, 1983–1993: California, Illinois, Michigan, New York, and Texas—An update from the Multistate Foster Care Data Archive.* Chicago: Chapin Hall Center for Children, University of Chicago.

Goldsmith, D. J. (1995). Individual vs. collective rights: The Indian Child Welfare Act. *Harvard Women's Law Journal, 13*, 4.

Gravel, R. & Roberge, P. (1984). *Le vecu en adoption internacionale au Quebec.* Quebec City, PQ: Ministere des Affaires Sociales.

Gray Eyes, D. (1995). Establishing Status of Indian Children: Hearings on S. 1448 Before the House Subcommittee on Native American and Insular Affairs, 104th Congress.

Grotevant, H. D. (1988). The rise and fall of transracial adoption: Science meets politics. *Contemporary Psychology, 33*(10), 853–855.

Grow, L. J. & Shapiro, D. (1974). *White parents: A study of transracial adoption.* New York: CWLA.

Guerrero, M. P. (1979). Indian Child Welfare Act of 1978: A response to the threat to Indian culture caused by foster and adoptive placements of Indian children. *American Indian Law Review, 7*, 51–77.

Gunnarby, A., Hofvander, Y., Sjolin, S., & Sundelin, C. (1982). Utlandska adoptivbarns halsotillstand och anpassning till svenska forhallanden. *Larkartidningen, 79*(17), 1697–1705.

Harden, A. W., Clark, R. L., & McGuire, K. (1997). *Informal and formal kinship care.* Chicago: Chapin Hall Center for Children.

Harder, E. (1987). *International adoption: An exploration of how adolescents are faring.* M.S.W. Thesis, Wilfrid Laurier University, Waterloo, Ontario.

Harrison, A. O. (1996). Comments on transracial adoption. *Journal of Black Psychology, 22,* 236–239.

Harvey, I. (1983). Adoption of Vietnamese children: An Australian study. *Australian Journal of Social Issues, 18*(1), 35–42.

Haven, P. (1999, May 4). Many hurdles to adopting Kosovars. *Associated Press.* [On-line]. Available: http://www.dailynews.yahoo.com/headlines.

Hayes, P. (1993). Transracial adoption; Politics and ideology. *Child Welfare, 72,* 301–310.

Hayes, P. (1995). The ideological attack on transracial adoption in the USA and Britain. *International Journal of Law and the Family, 9,* 1–22.

Hegar, R. L., & Scannapieco, M. (1995). From family duty to family policy: The evolution of kinship care. *Child Welfare, 74,* 200–216.

Hester, M. (1999, April 20). Personal communication. Director, International Adoption, The Barker Foundation, Washington, DC.

Hewins, K. P. & Webster, L. J. (1927). *The work of child-placing agencies.* Washington, DC: U.S. Children's Bureau.

Hill, R. B. (1972). *The strengths of black families* (2nd ed.). New York: National Urban League.

Hill, R. B. (1977). *Informal adoption among black families.* Washington, DC: National Urban League.

Hill, R. B. (1981, 1993). Black pulse survey. Washington, DC: National Urban League.

Hill, R. B. (1993). *Research on the African-American family.* Westport, CT: Auburn House.

Hill, R. B. (1997). *The strengths of African American families: Twenty-five years later.* Washington, DC: R & B Publishers.

Hill, R. B. (In press). Black kin caregivers and child welfare issues: Research implications. In R. P. Barth, M. Freundlich, & D. Brodzinsky (Eds.), *Adoption and prenatal alcohol and drug exposure: Research, practice and policy.* Washington, DC: CWLA Press.

Hodges, L. (1996, July 19). Blood ties. *New York Times,* p. A27.

Hofvander, Y. Bengtsson, E., Gunnarby, A., Cederblad, M., Kats, M. & Stromholm, S. (1978). U-landsadotivbarn-halsa och anpassning. *Lakartidningen, 75*, 4673–4680.

Hogan, P. & Siu, S. (1988). Minority children and the child welfare system: An historical perspective. *Social Work, 37*, 493–498.

Hoksbergen, R. A. C. (1987). *Adopted children at home and at school: The integration after eight years of 116 Thai children in the Dutch society.* Lisse, Netherlands: Swets & Zeitlinger B.V.

Hoksbergen, R. A. C. (1991). Understanding and preventing "failing adoptions." In E. Hibbs (Ed.), *Adoptions: International perspectives* (pp. 265–279). New York: International Universities.

Hollinger, J. H. (n.d.). *Beyond the best interests of the tribe: Determining children's "identity" under the Indian Child Welfare Act. A Comment on* Bridget R. v. Cindy R. On file with The Evan B. Donaldson Adoption Institute.

Hollinger, J. H. (1989). Beyond the best interests of the tribe: The Indian Child Welfare Act and the adoption of Indian children. *University of Detroit Law Review, 66*, 451–501.

Hollingsworth, L. D. (1998). Promoting same-race adoption for children of color. *Social Work, 43*, 104–116.

Holt International Families. (1999, March/April). Striving for integrity. *HI Families, 7.*

Hopson, D. P. & Hopson, D. S. (1990). *Different and wonderful: Raising black children in a race-conscious society.* New York: Prentice Hall Press.

Horejsi, C. R. (1987). *Child welfare practice and the Native American family in Montana: A handbook for social workers.* Missoula: Department of Social Work, University of Montana (Mimeograph).

Horejsi, C., Craig, B. H. R., & Pablo, J. (1992). Reactions by Native American parents to child protection agencies: Cultural and community factors. *Child Welfare, 71*, 329–341.

Hornby, H., Zeller, D., & Karraker, D. (1996). Kinship care in America: What outcomes should policy seek? *Child Welfare, 75*, 397–418.

Howard, M. (1984). Transracial adoption: Analysis of the best interests standard. *Notre Dame Law Review, 59*, 503–555.

Howe, R. A. W. (1997). Transracial adoption (TRA): Old prejudices and discrimination float under a new halo. *The Boston University Public Interest Law Journal, 6*(2), 409–472.

Huh, N. S. (1997). Korean children's ethnic identity formation and understanding of adoption. Ph.D. Dissertation, State University of New York at Albany.

Ingram, C. (1996). Kinship care: Last resort to first choice. *Child Welfare, 75,* 550–566.

In re Adoption of Baby Boy L. (1982). 643 P.2d 168 (Kansas).

In re Adoption of a Child of Indian Heritage. (1988). 543 A.2d 925 (New Jersey).

In re Adoption of T.N.F. (1989). 781 P.2d 973 (Alaska).

In re Adoption of T.R.M. v. D.R.L. (1988). 525 N.E.2d 298 (Indiana), cert denied, 490 U.S. 1069 (1989).

In re J.J.S. (1983). No. WR-CV-21-83, Nav.D. Window Rock, 11, Indian L. Rep. 6031.

In re Stephanie M. (1994). 7 Cal. App. 4th 295.

In the Adoption of Lindsay C. (1991). 280 Cal. Rptr. 194.

In the Matter of Baby Boy Doe. (1993). 849 P.2d 925, 931 (Idaho).

In the Matter of the Welfare of D.L. (1992). 486 N.W.2d 375 (Minnesota).

Indian Child Welfare Act (1978). 25 U.S.C. §§ 1901–1923.

Interethnic Placement Act Amendments of 1996, Pub. L. No. 104-188 (1996).

Issac, C. (1978). Tribal Chief of the Mississippi Band of Choctaw Indians. Hearings on S. 1214 before the Subcommittee on Indian Affairs and Public Lands of the House Committee on Interior and Insular Affairs, 95th Cong., 2nd Session.

Jackson-White, G., Dozier, C. D., Oliver, J. T., & Gardner, L. B. (1997). Why African American adoption agencies succeed: A new perspective on self-help. *Child Welfare, 76,* 239–254.

Jeter, H. (1963). *Children, problems, and services in child welfare programs.* (Children's Bureau Publication No. 403-1963). Washington, DC: U.S. Department of Health, Education, and Welfare.

Joe, B. (1978). In defense of intercountry adoption. *Social Service Review, 53,* 1–20.

Johnson, P. R., Shireman, J. F., & Watdon, K. W. (1987). Transracial adoption and the development of black identity at age eight. *Child Welfare, 66,* 45–55.

Jones, C. (1993, October 24). Role of race in adoptions: Old debate is being reborn. *The New York Times,* p. A1.

Jones, M. (1992). Adoption agencies: Can they service African Americans? *Crisis, 8,* 26–28.

Kamerman, S. B. (1998/1999). Child welfare and the under-threes: An overview. *Zero to Three Bulletin, 19*(3), 1, 3–7.

Kansas Statutes Annotated. (1993). Sections 83-1584.

Katz, L. (1999). Concurrent planning: Benefits and pitfalls. *Child Welfare, 78,* 71–87.

Kellogg Foundation. (n.d.). *Families for kids of color: A special report on challenges and opportunities.* Battle Creek, MI: W.W. Kellogg Foundation.

Keltie, P. (1969). *The adjustment of Korean children adopted by couples in the Chicago area.* M.S.W. Thesis, Jane Addams School of Social Work, University of Illinois,Chicago.

Kennedy, R. (1994). Orphans of separatism: The painful politics of transracial adoption. *The American Prospect, 17,* 38–45.

Kennedy, R. (1998). Testimony before the Subcommittee on Human Resources of the House Committee on Ways and Means. Hearing on Interethnic Adoptions. September 15. [On-line]. Available: www.house.gov/ways_means/humres/testmony/9-15-98/9-15kenn.htm

Khinduka, S. K. (1995). Ethnic conflicts: Can anything be done? *Social Development Issues, 17*(1), 1–17.

Kim, D. S. (1976). *Intercountry adoptions: A study of adolescent self-concept formation of Korean children who were adopted in American families.* Ph.D. dissertation, University of Chicago.

Kim, D. S. (1977). How they fared in American homes: A follow-up study of adopted Korean children in the United States. *Children Today, 6,* 2–6, 36.

Kim, D. S. (1978). Issues in transracial and transcultural adoption. *Social Casework, 5,* 477–486.

Kim, P. S. (1980). Behaviour symptoms in three transracially adopted Asian children: Diagnosis dilemma. *Child Welfare, 59,* 213–224.

Kim, P. S., Hong, S., & Kim B. S. (1979). Adoption of Korean children by New York area couples: A preliminary study. *Child Welfare, 58,* 419–427.

Kim, W. J. (1995). International adoption: A case review of Korean children. *Child Psychiatry and Human Development, 25*(3), 141–154.

Kirk, H. D. (1984). *Shared Fate: A theory and method of adoptive relationships.* Port Angeles, WA: Ben-Simon Publications.

Kossoudji, S. A. (1989). Pride and predjudice: Culture's role in markets. In S. Shulman & W. Darity (Eds.), *The question of discrimination: Racial inequality in the U.S. labor market* (pp. 293–314). Middletown, CT: Wesleyan University Press.

Kramer, R. (1994, October 24). Adoption in black and white. *The Wall Street Journal,* p. 23.

Kroll, J. (1998). Testimony before the Subcommittee on Human Resources of the House Committee on Ways and Means. Hearing on Interethnic Adoptions. September 15. [On-line]. Available: www.house.gov/ ways_means/humres/testmony/9-15-98/9-15krol.htm

Kuhl, W. (1985). *When adopted children of foreign origin grow up.* Osnabruck, ON: Terre des Hommes.

Kunesh P. H. (1996). Transcending frontiers: Indian child welfare in the United States. *Boston College Third World Law Journal, 16,* 17–34.

Kusserow, R. P. (1991). *Barriers to freeing children for adoption.* Washington, DC: U.S. Department of Health and Human Services, Office of the Inspector General.

Langsam, M. Z. (1964). *Children west: A history of the placing-out system of the New York Children's Aid Society 1853–1890.* Madison: University of Wisconsin.

Lehmann, D. J. (1999, March 17). Baby T ruling gets attention. *Chicago Sun Times.* [On-line]. Available: www.suntimes.com:80/output/ news/fed17i.html.

Lin, J. (1998, December 23). Beijing eases adoption rules to aid abandoned babies. *San Jose Mercury News.* [On-line]. Available: http://www7.mercurycenter.com:80/premium/world/docs/ asia23.html.

Linowitz, J. & Boothby, N. (1988). Cross-cultural placements. In E. Ressler, N. Boothby, & D. Steinbock (Eds.), *Unaccompanied children: Care and protection in wars, natural disasters, and refugee movements* (pp. 181–207). New York: Oxford University Press.

Logan, S. L. (1981). Race, identity and black children: A developmental perspective. *Social Casework, 62,* 47–56.

Lorde, A. (1984). *Sister outsider: Essays and speeches*. Trumansburg, NY: Crossing Press.

Lum, D. (1986). *Social work practice and people of color: A process-stage approach*. Monterey, CA: Brooks/Cole.

MacEachron, A. E., Gustavsson, N. S., Cross, S., & Lewis, A. (1996). The effectiveness of the Indian Child Welfare Act of 1978. *Social Service Review, 70*, 451–463.

McCarthy, C. (1996, July 16). Reopening the drain on Indians' Legacy. *Washington Post*, p. B8.

McCarthy, R. J. (1993). The Indian Child Welfare Act: In the best interests of the child and tribe. *Clearinghouse Review, 27*, 864–873.

McKelvey, C. & Stevens, J. (1994). *Adoption crisis: The truth behind adoption and foster care*. Golden, CO: Fulcrum.

McKenzie, J. (1993). Adoption of children with special needs. *The Future of Children, 3*(1), 62–76.

McIntosh, P. (1997). White privilege: Unpacking the invisible knapsack. In B. Schneider (Ed.), *Race: An anthology in the first person* (pp. 120–126). New York: Three Rivers Press.

McRoy, R. (1989). An organizational dilemma: The case of transracial adoptions. *Journal of Applied Behavioral Science, 25*, 145–160.

McRoy, R. G. (1991). Significance of ethnic and racial identity in inter-country adoption within the United States. *Adoption and Fostering, 15*(4), 53–61.

McRoy, R. G. (1994). Attachment and racial identity issues: Implications for child placement decision making. *Journal of Multicultural Social Work, 3*(3), 59–74.

McRoy, R. G. (1996). Racial identity issues for Black children in foster care. In S. L. Logan (Ed.), *The black family: Strengths, self-help and positive change* (pp. 131–143). Boulder, CO: Westview Press.

McRoy, R. G., Oglesby, Z., & Grape, H. (1997). Achieving same-race adoptive placements for African American children: Culturally sensitive practice approaches. *Child Welfare, 76*, 85–106.

McRoy, R. G. & Zurcher, L. (1983). *Transracial and inracial adoptees: The adolescent years*. Springfield, IL: Charles Thomas Publishers.

McRoy, R. G., Zurcher, L. A., Lauderdale, M. L., & Anderson, R. E. (1982). Self-esteem and racial identity in transracial and inracial adoptees. *Social Work, 27*, 522–526.

McRoy, R. G., Zurcher, L. A., Lauderdale, M. L., & Anderson, R. E. (1984). The identity of transracial adoptees. *Social Casework, 65*, 34–39.

Mahoney, J. (1991). The black baby doll: Transracial adoption and cultural preservation. *University of Missouri Kansas City Law Review, 59*, 487–501.

Mannes, M. (1990). *Leadership in administering Indian human services.* Las Cruces: New Mexico State University.

Mannes, M. (1993). Seeking the balance between child protection and family preservation in Indian child welfare. *Child Welfare, 72*, 141–150.

Mascareñas, D. (1997). The Latino child in transracial adoptions. In S. K. Roszia, A. Baran, & L. Coleman (Eds.), *Creating kinship* (pp. 101–113). Portland: Edmund S. Muskie School of Public Service, University of Southern Maine.

Mason, J. & Williams, C. (1985). The adoption of minority children: Issues in developing law and policy. In *Adoption of children with special needs: Issues in law and policy* (pp.81–93). Washington, DC: American Bar Association.

Matheson, L. (1996). The politics of the Indian Child Welfare Act. *Social Work, 41*, 232–235.

Maza, P. (2000, March 28). *The latest from AFCARS on adoptions and waiting children.* Presentation at the Children's Bureau Sixth National Child Welfare Conference, "Celebrating Innovation and Leadership in Child Welfare Services," Arlington, VA.

Meezan, W., Katz, S., & Russo, E. M. (1978). *Adoptions without agencies: A study of independent adoptions.* New York: Child Welfare League of America.

Melchoior, T. (1986). Adoption in Denmark. In R. Hoksbergen (Ed.), *Adoption in worldwide perspective* (pp. 211–220). Berwyn, PA: Swets North America, Inc.

Melone, T. (1976). Adoption and crisis in the Third World: Thoughts on the future. *International Child Welfare Review, 29*, 20–25.

Merritt, W. T. (1985). Excerpt from testimony by William T. Merritt, President of the National Association of Black Social Workers, during U.S. Senate Hearings of the Committee on Labor and Human Resources, June 25, 1985.

Metzenbaum, H. M. (1995). S. 1224—In Support of Multiethnic Placement Act of 1993. *Duke Journal of Gender Law and Policy, 2,* 165–172.

Mindel, C. H. & Habenstein, R. W. (1981). Family lifestyles of America's ethnic minorities: An introduction. In C. H. Mindel & R. W. Habenstein (Eds.), *Ethnic families in America: Patterns and variations* (pp. 1–12). New York: Elsevier.

Minnesota Statutes Annotated. (1995). Section 259.29.

Mississippi Band of Choctaw Indians v. Holyfield. (1989). 490 U.S. 30.

Mittleberg, D. & Waters, M. (1992). The process of enthogenesis among Haitian and Israeli immigrants in the United States. *Ethnic and Racial Studies, 15,* 412–435.

Model Children's Court Advisory Committee. (1998). *Essex County, New Jersey: Implementation of New Guidelines.* On file with the Evan B. Donaldson Adoption Institute.

Modell, J. S. (1994). *Kinship with strangers: Adoption and interpretations of kinship in American culture.* Berkeley: University of California Press.

Montiel, M. & Wong, P. (1983). A theoretical critique of the minority perspective. *Social Casework, 64,* 112–117.

Morgenstern, J. (1971, September 13). The new face of adoption. *Newsweek,* 67–72.

Morton, T. (1993). Ideas in action: The issue is race. *Child Welfare Institute Newsletter,* 1–2.

Mosher, W. D. & Bachrach, C. A. (1996). Understanding U.S. fertility: Continuity and change in the National Survey of Family Growth. *Family Planning Perspectives, 28*(1), 4–12.

Multi-Ethnic Placement Act of 1994, Pub. L. No. 103-382 (1994).

Murphy, P. (1998). Testimony before the Subcommittee on Human Resources of the House Committee on Ways and Means. Hearing on Interethnic Adoptions. September 15. [On-line]. Available: www.house.gov/ways_means/humres/testmony/9-15-98/9-15murp.htm

Mussen, P. H., Conger, J., & Kagan, J. (1969). *Child Development and Personality* (2nd ed). New York: Harper & Row.

Myer, R. & James, R. K. (1989). Internationally adopted children: A personal intervention approach. *Elementary School Guidance and Counseling, 23*(4), 324–330.

Nadel, M. (1998). Testimony before the Subcommittee on Human Resources of the House Committee on Ways and Means. Hearing on
Interethnic Adoptions. September 15. [On-line]. Available:
www.house.gov/ways_means/humres/testmony/9-15-98/9-
15nade.htm

National Association of Black Social Workers. (1972). *Position paper:
Transracial adoption.* New York: National Association of Black
Social Workers.

National Association of Black Social Workers. (1994). *Position statement: Preserving African American families.* Detroit, MI: National
Association of Black Social Workers.

National Association of Black Social Workers. (1996). *Focal point:
The case against transracial adoption.* [On-line]. Available: http://
www.adm.pdx.edu/user/rri/rtc/tp/transrac.htm.

National Black Child Development Institute. (1989). *Who will care when
parents can't? A study of black children in foster care.* Washington,
DC: National Black Child Development Institute.

National Center for Health Statistics. (1997). Fertility, family planning,
and women's health: New data from the 1995 National Survey of
Family Growth. *Vital Health Statistics, 23*(19).

National Council for Adoption. (1997). Racism in adoption: Is it gone?
National Adoption Reports, 18(8), 6.

Native American Children and Family Services Institute. (n.d.). *Curriculum for foster parenting Native Americans.* Bismarck, North Dakota.

Ngabonziza, D. (1988). Intercountry adoption: In whose best interest?
Adoption and Fostering, 12(1), 35–40.

Nishi, S. M. (1989). Perceptions and deceptions: Contemporary views of
Asian-Americans. In G. Yun (Ed.), *A look beyond the model minor-
ity image: Critical issues in Asian America* (pp. 3–10). New York:
Minority Rights Group, Inc.

Omi, M. & Winant, H. (1994). *Racial formation in the United States.* New
York: Routledge.

Oppenheim, L. & Bussiere, A. (1996). Adoption: Where do relatives
stand? *Child Welfare, 75,* 471–488.

Organization of American States. (1984). Convencion Interamericana
sobre conflictos de leyes en materia de adopcion. Third Specialized
Interamerican Conference on International Private Law. *La Paz,* 15.

Ortega, R. M., Guillean, C., & Najera, L. G. (1996). *Latinos and child welfare: Voces de la comunidad.* Ann Arbor: The University of Michigan.

Ortiz, F. (1998, December 3). Guatemala to reform adoption procedures. *Sun Sentinel*, p. 13A.

Otto, M. (1999, May 2). Kosovo kids "not adoptable." *San Jose Mercury News.* [On-line]. Available at: http://www.mercurycenter.com:80/premium/world/docs/orphans02.htm.

Pelton, L. (1994). Is poverty a key contributor to child maltreatment? In D. Gambrill & T. J. Stein (Eds.), *Controversial issues in child welfare* (pp. 16–28). Needham Heights, MA: Allyn and Bacon.

Perlez, J. (1994, Oct. 27). No love and little care: Romania's sad orphans. *New York Times*, p. 4.

Perry, T. L. (1990/1991). Race and child placement: The best interests test and the cost of discretion. *Journal of Family Law, 29*, 51–127.

Perry, T. L. (1993/1994). The transracial adoption controversy: An analysis of discourse and subordination. *NYU Review of Law and Social Change, 21*(3), 34–107.

Peters, M. F. (1985). Racial socialization of young black children. In B. H. McAdoo & J. L. McAdoo (Eds.), *Black children: Social, educational and parental environments* (pp.159–173). Beverly Hills, CA: Sage Publications.

Phinney, J. S. (1990). Ethnic identity in adolescents and adults: Review of research. *Psychological Bulletin, 108*, 499–514.

Phinney, J. S. (1991). Ethnic identity and self-esteem: A review and integration. *Hispanic Journal of Behavioral Sciences, 13*, 171–183.

Phinney, J. S. & Alipuria, L. L. (1990). Ethnic identity in college students from four ethnic groups. *Journal of Adolescence, 13*, 171–183.

Phinney, J. S., Lochner, B. T., & Murphy, R. (1990). Ethnic identity development and psychological adjustment in adolescence. In A. R. Stiffman & L. E. Davis (Eds.), *Ethnic issues in adolescent mental health* (pp. 53–72). Newbury Park, CA: Sage Publications.

Phinney, J. S. & Rosenthal, D.A. (1992). Ethnic identity in adolescence: Process, content and outcome. In G. Adams, T. Gullotta, & R. Montemayor (Eds.), *Adolescent identity formation* (pp.145–172). Newbury Park, CA: Sage.

Pierce, W. (1998). Testimony before the Subcommittee on Human Resources of the House Committee on Ways and Means. Hearing on

Interethnic Adoptions. September 15. [On-line]. Available: www.house.gov/ways_means/humres/testmony/9-15-98/9-15pierce.htm

Pinderhughes, E. (1989). *Understanding race, ethnicity and power: The key to efficacy in clinical practice.* New York: The Free Press.

Plantz, M. C., Hubbell, R., Barrett, B. J., & Dobrec, A. (1988). *Indian child welfare: A status report—final report of the survey of Indian child welfare and implementation of the Indian Child Welfare Act and section 428 of the Adoption Assistance and Child Welfare Act of 1980.* CSR Incorporated and Three Feathers Associates (105-82-1602). Washington, DC: U.S. Department of Health and Human Services, Administration on Children, Youth and Families, U.S. Department of the Interior, Bureau of the Indian Affairs.

Pohl, C. & Harris, K. (1992). *Transracial adoption: Children and parents speak.* New York: Franklin Watts.

Pollack, I. (1998, November 5). Presentation: MEPA/IPA. Annual Conference of the Association of Administrators of the Interstate Compact on Adoption and Medical Assistance. Oklahoma City, OK.

Proshansky, H. (1965). *Basic studies in social psychology.* New York: Rinehart & Winston.

Pruzan, V. (1977). Born in a foreign country—adopted in Denmark. *International Child Welfare Review, 36*(2), 41–47.

Pryce, D. (1995). Establishing Status of Indian Children: Hearings on S. 1448 Before the House Subcommittee on Native American and Insular Affairs, 104th Congress.

Quinn v. Walters. (1993). 845 P.2d 206 (Oregon).

Rathburn, C., McLaughlin, H., Bennett, C., & Garland, J. (1965). Later adjustment of children following radical separation from family and culture. *American Journal of Orthopsychiatry, 35*, 604–609.

Reitman, V. (1999, March 6). S. Korea tries to take care of its own with domestic adoptions. *Los Angeles Times.* Available: www.latimes.com.80/excite/990306/t00002045.1.html.

Rios-Kohn, R. (1998). Intercountry adoption: An international perspective on the practice and standards. *Adoption Quarterly, 1*(4), 3–32.

Risling, M. J. (1998). *The bench book.* Eureka, CA: California Indian Legal Services.

Rodriguez, P. & Meyer, A. (1990). Minority adoptions and agency practices. *Social Work, 35*, 528–531.

Rorbech, M. (1991). The conditions of 18-to-25 year old foreign born adoptees in Denmark. In H. Alstein & R. J. Simon (Eds.), *Intercountry adoption: A multinational perspective* (pp. 127–140). New York: Praeger.

Ross, E. L. (1978). *Black heritage in social welfare 1860–1930.* Metuchen, NJ: Scarecrow Press, Inc.

Rotheram, M. J. & Phinney, J. S. (1987). Ethnic behavior as patterns as an aspect of identity. In J. S. Phinney & M. J. Rotheram (Eds.), *Children's ethnic socialization: Pluralism and development* (pp. 201–218). Newbury Park, CA: Sage Publications.

Rushton, A. & Minnis, H. (1997). Annotation: Trans-racial family placements. *Journal of Child Psychology and Psychiatry and Allied Disciplines, 38,* 147–159.

Ryan, A. S. (1983). Intercountry adoption and policy issues. *Journal of Children in Contemporary Society, 15*(3), 49–60.

Saetersdal, B. & Dalen, M. (1991). Norway: Intercountry adoptions in a homogeneous country. In H. Altstein & R. J. Simon (Eds.), *Intercountry adoption: A multinational perspective* (pp. 83–108). New York: Praeger.

Schoof, R. (1999, April 21). More baby girls abandoned in China. *Associated Press.* [On-line]. Available: http://dailynews.yahoo.com/ headlin...990421/wl/china_abandonment_l.html.

Semaj, L.T. (1985). Afrikanity, cognition and extended self-identity. In M. B. Spencer, G. K. Brookins, & W. R. Allen (Eds.), *Beginnings: The social and affective development of Black children* (pp. 173–183). Hillsdale, NJ: Lawrence Erlbaum Publishers.

Sheindlin, J. B. (1994, August 29). Paying grandmas to keep kids in limbo. *The New York Times,* p. A25 (op-ed).

Shireman, J. & Johnson, P. (1988). *Growing up adopted.* Chicago: Chicago Child Care Society.

Silverman, A. R. (1993). Outcomes of transracial adoption. *The Future of Children, 3*(1), 104–118.

Simon, R. J. & Altstein, H. (1977). *Transracial adoption.* New York: John Wiley and Sons.

Simon, R. J. & Altstein, H. (1981). *Transracial adoption: A followup.* Lexington, MA: Lexington Books.

Simon, R. J. & Altstein, H. (1987). *Transracial adoptees and their families: A study of identity and commitment.* New York: Praeger.

Simon, R. J. & Altstein, H. (1992). *Adoption, race, and identity: From infancy through adolescence.* New York: Praeger.

Simon, R., Altstein, H., & Melli, M. (1994). *The case for transracial adoption.* Washington, DC: American University Press.

Small, J. (1984). The crisis in adoption. *The International Journal of Social Psychiatry, 30,* 129–42.

Smith, A. & Stewart, A. J. (1973). Approaches to studying racism and sexism in black women's lives. *Journal of Social Issues, 39,* 1–15.

Smith, J. (1988, July 3). Young once, Indian forever. *Image,* 3–11.

Smolowe, J. (1994, August 22). Babies for export. *Time,* 65–66.

Spence Chapin Adoption Services. (1947). *The Spence Chapin Adoption Services Annual Report.* New York: Spence Chapin.

Stack, C. (1974). *All our kin: Stategies for survival in a black community.* New York: Harper and Row.

Stanley, A. (1997, June 29). Hands off our babies: A Georgian tells America. *New York Times,* p. E1.

Stehno, S. (1990). The elusive continuum of child welfare services: Implications for minority children and youths. *Child Welfare, 69,* 551–562.

Stolley, K. S. (1993). Statistics on adoption in the United States. *The Future of Children, 3,* 26–42.

Stonequist, E. V. (1935). The problem of marginal man. *American Journal of Sociology, 7,* 1–12.

Sussman, A. & Guggenheim, M. (1980). *The rights of parents: The basic ACLU guide to the rights of parents* (An American Civil Liberties Union handbook). New York: Avon.

Takaki, R. (1987). *From different shores.* New York: Oxford University Press.

Takaki, R. (1989). *Strangers from a different shore: A history of Asian Americans.* Boston: Little, Brown & Co.

Tatara, T. (1993). *Voluntary Cooperative Information System (VCIS), Characteristics of children in substitute and adoptive care [based on FY 82 through FY 90 data].* Washington, DC: American Public Welfare Association.

Taylor, R. J. & Thornton, M. C. (1996). Child welfare and transracial adoption. *Journal of Black Psychology, 22,* 282–291.

Teicher, S. A. (1999, April 14). Fight over mixed race adoption. *The Christian Science Monitor.* [On-line]. Available: h t t p : / / w w w . c s m o n i t o r . c o m / a t c s m o n i t o r / s...hmonth/news/p-041499adoptions.html].

Testa, M. F., Shook, K. L., Cohen, L. S., & Woods, M. G. (1996). Permanency planning options for children in formal kinship care. *Child Welfare, 75,* 451–470.

Thompson, E. L. (1990). Protecting abused children: A judge's perspective on public law deprived child proceedings and the impact of the Indian Child Welfare Act. *American Indian Law Review, 15*(1), 10.

Thorne, W. (1999, June 7). Personal communication with Judge W. Thorne, State Court Judge, State of Utah and Tribal Court Judge.

Thurston, A. F. (1996). In a Chinese orphanage. *The Atlantic Monthly, 277*(4), 28–41.

Tizard, B. (1991). Intercountry adoption: A review of the evidence. *Journal of Child Psychology and Psychiatry, 32,* 743–56.

Tolfree, D. (1978). Problems of intercountry adoption. *Social Work Today, 10*(13), 16–18.

Triseliotis, J. (1991). Intercountry adoption: A brief overview of the research evidence. *Adoption and Fostering, 15*(4), 46–52.

Triseliotis, J. (1993). Inter-country adoption: In whose best interest? In M. Humphrey & H. Humphrey (Eds.), *Inter-country adoption: Practical experiences* (pp.129–137). London: Routledge.

Trolley, B. C., Wallin, J., & Hansen, J. (1995). International adoption: Acknowledgement of adoption and birth culture. *Child and Adolescent Social Work Journal, 12,* 465–479.

Tuan, Mia. (in press). *Forever foreigners or honorary whites?: The Asian ethnic experience today.* New Brunswick: Rutgers University Press.

University of Iowa. (1993). *Family functioning of neglectful families.* Des Moines: University of Iowa.

U.S. Bureau of the Census. (1998). Current Population Reports, Series P-25, No. 311, *Estimates of the Population of the United States by Single Years of Age, Color, and Sex: 1900 to 1959*; Series P-25, No. 519, *Estimates of the Population of the United States by Single Years of Age, Sex and Race: April 1, 1960 to July 1, 1973*; Series P-25, No. 917, Preliminary *Estimates of the Population of the United States by*

Single Years of Age, Sex and Race: 1970 to 1981; Series P-25, No. 1130, *Population Projections of the united States by Age, Sex, Race, and Hispanic Origin: 1995 to 2050.*

U.S. Department of Health and Human Services. (2000). *AFCARS Data: Current estimates as of January 2000.* [On-line]. Available: http://www.acf.dhhs.gov/programs/cb/stats/tarreport/rpt0100/ar0100.htm.

U.S. Department of State. (1999). Immigrant visas issued to orphans coming to the U.S. [On-line]. Available: http://travel.state.gov/orphan_numbers.html.

U.S. General Accounting Office. (1994). *Foster care: Parental drug abuse has alarming impact on young children.* Washington, DC: U.S. General Accounting Office.

U.S. House of Representatives Report. (1978). No. 1386, 95th Congress, 2nd Session, at 9.

U.S. Information Agency. (1994). *The "baby parts" myth: The anatomy of a rumor.* Washington, DC: United States Information Agency.

U.S. National Center for Health Statistics. (1990). Adoption in the 1980's. *Advance Data* 181 [January 5]. Washington DC: U.S. Government Printing Office.

U. S. Senate Report. (1977). Hearing on S. 1214 before the Senate Select Committee on Indian Affairs. 95th Congress, 1st Session 43.

Vega, W. A., Kolody, B., Hwang, J., & Noble, A. (1993). Prevalence and magnitude of perinatal substance exposure in California. *New England Journal of Medicine, 12,* 850–54.

Verhulst, F. C., Althus, M., & Versluis-den Bieman, H. J. M. (1990). Problem behaviour in international adoptees: 1. An epidemiological study. *Journal of the American Academy of Child and Adolescent Psychiatry. 29,* 94–111.

Versluis-den Bieman, H. J. M. & Verhulst, F. C. (1995). Self-reported and parent reported problems in adolescent international adoptees. *Journal of Child Psychology and Psychiatry, 36,* 1411–1428.

Villanueva, M. (1990, December 25). A preliminary report outlining the available research and current theoretical thinking on extra-cultural adoption and extra-cultural foster care placement of American Indian children. Technical report prepared for the Foster Care Unit of the Urban Indian Child Resource Center, Oakland, CA.

Vroegh, K. S. (1997). Transracial adoptees: Developmental status after 17 years. *American Journal of Orthopsychiatry, 67*, 568–575.

Walters, R. W. (1982). Race, resources, conflict. *Social Work, 27*, 24–30.

Warner, W. L. & Srole, L. (1945). *The social systems of American ethnic groups.* New Haven, CT: Yale University Press.

Waters, M. C. (1986). *The process and content of ethnic identification: A study of white ethnics in suburbia (Irish, Italian, Polish, Portuguese, California).* Ph.D. dissertation, University of California, Berkeley.

Waters, M. C. (1990). *Ethnic options: Choosing identities in America.* Berkeley: University of California Press.

Waters, M. C. (1992). The construction of symbolic ethnicity: Suburban white ethnics in the 1980's. In M. D'Innocenzo & J.P. Sirefman (Eds.), *Immigration and ethnicity: American society—"melting pot" or "salad bowl"?* (pp. 75–90). Westport, CT: Greenwood Press.

Watkins, K. (1987). *Parent-child attachment.* New York: Garland Publishing.

Watts, S. (1989). Voluntary adoptions under the Indian Child Welfare Act of 1978: Balancing the interests of children, families, and tribes. *Southern California Law Review, 63*, 213–256.

Weil, R. H. (1984). International adoption: The quiet migration. *International Migration Review, 18*, 280–281.

Westermeyer, J. (1974). Indian Child Welfare Program: Hearings before the Subcommittee on Indian Affairs of the Senate Committee on Interior and Insular Affairs, 93rd Congress, 2nd Session.

Westermeyer, J. (1979). The Apple Syndrome in Minnesota: A complication of racial-ethnic discontinuity. *Journal of Operational Psychology, 10*, 134–140.

Westhues, A. & Cohen, J. S. (1994). *Intercountry adoption in Canada: Final report.* Toronto, ON: National Human Resources Development Canada, Welfare Grants Division.

Wilkinson, H. (1981). *Birth is more than once: The inner world of adopted Korean children.* Ph.D. dissertation. Ann Arbor, MI: Microfilms International.

Wilkinson, H. S. (1995). Psycholegal process and issues in international adoption. *American Journal of Family Therapy, 23*, 173–183.

Williams, C. (1991). Expanding the options in the quest for permanence. In J. E. Everett, S. S. Chipungu, & B. R. Leashore (Eds.), *Child welfare: An Africentric perspective* (pp. 266–289). New Brunswick, NJ: Rutgers University Press.

Willis, M. G. (1996). The real issues in transracial adoption: A response. *Journal of Black Psychology, 22,* 246–253.

Yavapai-Apache v. Mejia. (1995). 906 S.W.2d 152 (Texas).

About the Author

Madelyn Freundlich is the executive director of The Evan B. Donaldson Adoption Institute. She is a social worker and lawyer whose work has focused on child welfare policy and practice for the past decade. She formerly served as general counsel for the Child Welfare League of America and as associate director of Program and Planning for the Massachusetts Society for the Prevention of Cruelty to Children. She is the author of a number of books and articles on child welfare law, policy, and financing. Her most recent writing has focused on the impact of welfare reform on foster care and special-needs adoption, interstate adoption law and practice, genetic testing in adoption evaluations, and confidentiality in adoption law and practice. Ms. Freundlich received her master's degrees in social work and public health, and she also holds a J.D. and LL.M.